WAGING
SPIRITUAL
WARFARE

WAGING SPIRITUAL WARFARE

RICHARD ING

WHITAKER
HOUSE

WAGING SPIRITUAL WARFARE:
PREPARING FOR THE FINAL CONFLICT AGAINST THE DEMONIC KINGDOM

Richard Ing
Light of the World Missions
P. O. Box 37451, Honolulu, HI 96837
www.lightoftheworldmissions.com

ISBN: 978-1-60374-022-7
Printed in the United States of America
© 2008 by Richard Ing

1030 Hunt Valley Circle
New Kensington, PA 15068
www.whitakerhouse.com

Library of Congress Cataloging-in Publication Data
Ing, Richard.
Waging spiritual warfare : preparing for the final conflict against the demonic kingdom / by Richard B.W. Ing.
p. cm.
Summary: "Details methods of inner healing as they relate to spiritual warfare, as well as a description of spiritual warfare in the end times"
—Provided by the publisher.
ISBN 978-1-60374-022-7 (trade pbk. : alk. paper)
1. Spiritual warfare. I. Title.
BV4509.5.I437 2008
235'.4—dc22   2007040491

3 4 5 6 7 8 9 10 11 **UJ** 15 14 13 12 11 10 09

CONTENTS

INTRODUCTION

As the end of the age swiftly approaches, the clash between God (the kingdom of light) and Satan (the kingdom of darkness) will intensify dramatically until the final battle between God's people and the children of the evil one takes place. (See Revelation 19:19–21.) Much of what we see in the physical realm has its counterpart in the spiritual realm and vice versa. What transpires in the spiritual determines many of our human events. Satan has battled against the kingdom of light for the souls of men, women, and children for thousands of years. As the present ruler of this world system, he has invaded and attempted to control every human endeavor and organization. Consequently, great portions of politics, business, education, medicine, law, military, entertainment, communications, and religion are under the influence of Satan's evil power.

While battles rage in the Middle East and other areas of the world, humans look to science, logic, politics, economics, and military strategies to attain victory and achieve peace. The Bible says, however,

> *For we do not wrestle against flesh and blood, but against principalities, against powers, against the rulers of the*

*darkness of this age, against spiritual hosts of wickedness in
the heavenly places.* (Ephesians 6:12)

This means that behind the seen wars and conflicts there
is a very real, yet unseen, spiritual war. As long as Satan's
ruler spirits or strongmen of hatred, anger, bitterness, revenge,
religiosity, deception, witchcraft, antichrist, murder, pride,
and greed are unchallenged, war and murder will continue
unabated.

Sadly, much of the church is woefully ignorant about
spiritual warfare, and Satan's demons have had their way
up until now. Most people within the body of Christ *do not*
wrestle at all.

Satan's greatest weapon is deception. Our Lord Jesus
Christ says that Satan will deceive the whole world. (See
Revelation 12:9.) Already, almost the entire body of Christ is
deceived and has become easy prey for Satan's demons. As
Jesus said, *"For false christs and false prophets will rise and show
great signs and wonders to deceive, if possible, even the elect"* (Matthew 24:24). In this book, I will attempt to expose some of the
deceptions and to further train and equip those who would
answer God's call to battle.

This book is arranged into two parts. Part One deals with
a number of aspects of spiritual deliverance not covered by
my first book, *Spiritual Warfare.* Part Two presents spiritual
warfare from the aspect of fighting for both revival and survival—the final global conflict against the demonic kingdom
and the battles soon to come.

Some of the topics may be considered controversial. Many
progressive Christians consider inner healing techniques too
close to occult practices, like visualization or imaging. After

much prayer and consultation with a number of wise and mature Christians, I have determined that Christians need to make up their own mind after learning certain facts about inner healing.

I will also present the topic of angels as a part of our weaponry in spiritual warfare. We are not alone in our battles against the forces of evil. God has assigned many angels to help fight against Satan's demonic kingdom and we need to know how to work with them. I have personally seen angels actively engaging in spiritual deliverance services.

Part Two of the book gives an overall view of the spiritual war going on today and a preview of the battles to come in the near future. What we see with our natural eyes is the product of ongoing activities in the spirit realm. The Bible tells us what to expect in our war with the kingdom of darkness and what Satan is doing.

It is axiomatic that the more you know about your enemy, the better prepared you are to engage him in battle and bring about his defeat. This book includes a formula for worldwide revival that can hopefully bring some unity to the body of Christ—at least to those who are willing to participate in it.

According to Scripture, many Christians will either renounce their faith or die in the end times. (See Matthew 24:8–12.) Satan's beast is going to war against the saints and overcome many of them. (See Revelation 13:6–7.) Only a remnant will make it through. That remnant will be fully mature in the Spirit and powerful in spiritual warfare. They will walk in God's ways.

I have occasionally met with fierce opposition from different parts of the body of Christ when speaking on the subject of deception. Given the success of Satan's lies and deceptions that have already infiltrated the body of Christ, it is understandable.

Deception is Satan's greatest weapon in his attempts to neutralize and destroy every Christian and church on earth. A part of the body of Christ has already bought into Satan's lies and will fight to defend them. Many will cling to Satan's lies until the very end and multitudes will fall. However, the good news is that God is raising up an army for the end times. This great army will engage in the greatest battle of all time against the kingdom of darkness.

In the end, the army of God will prevail!

PART ONE

SPIRITUAL DELIVERANCE

CHAPTER ONE

DEALING WITH THE GARBAGE

Satan's demons are attracted to spiritual garbage like flies. This is no coincidence. The Bible sometimes refers to Satan as Beelzebub. (See Matthew 12:24, 27; Luke 11:15, 18-19.) According to *Webster's New Collegiate Dictionary*, *Beelzebub* means the "Lord of the Flies."

The secret to getting rid of flies (demons) is to get rid of the garbage that attracts them—no garbage, no flies. Therefore, in deliverance our focus is not so much on killing flies as on garbage collection and disposal. Once it has been exposed and identified, we need to get rid of it!

The question, then, becomes, "What and where is the garbage?" Specifically, "garbage" refers to negative behaviors, attitudes, and outright lies that have settled into the life of a believer. This can take the form of repetitive sin patterns, addictions, and exposure to pornography or cultish material, as well as the unforgiveness and scars that come from past physical or mental abuse.

No matter how much you try, unless the garbage is removed, the enemy will return, even after a seemingly successful deliverance. You may be able to get the enemy out by pure persistence and spiritual power, but if the garbage remains, he will soon return. Just like shooing flies away, as soon as you stop, they come right back to the garbage.

This is why, even after a successful deliverance, some people do not seem to change significantly. Bad habits, attitudes, and behavior patterns persist. This is because the garbage remains, where it continues to stink and fester, triggering new sins of disobedience that attract Satan's demons back. The Lord Jesus alluded to this in Matthew 12:43–45:

> *When an unclean spirit goes out of a man, he goes through dry places, seeking rest, and finds none. Then he says, "I will return to my house from which I came." And when he comes, he finds it empty, swept, and put in order. Then he goes and takes with him seven other spirits more wicked than himself, and they enter and dwell there; and the last state of that man is worse than the first.*

The empty house may look pretty and sanitized, but until one fills the empty places with the Word of God and renews the mind, old attitudes and sin patterns can still lurk under the surface, leaving the door open for the demonic activity to return.

After a successful deliverance, one must establish new responses and emotions, as well as a new will, especially in the case of psychological or emotional problems. Fear, rejection, anger, bitterness, hatred, and similar spirits can leave for a time, but the emotional patterns that remain can lead the person back into negative or unacceptable behavior.

Dealing with the Garbage

George H. Kraft, in his book entitled *Defeating Dark Angels*, grades demon strength on a scale from one to ten. Those from six to ten are very powerful and will exhibit great resistance. Those from four to five are strong, but definitely manageable. Those in the one to three range are weaker and the first ones to leave during deliverance. It's simple: the weaker demons are, the easier they come out. Instead of directly taking on a demon in the six to ten range, simply take out the garbage first. According to Kraft, this reduces their strength, and they will depart more quickly.[1]

Establishing complete freedom from demons and their influence, therefore, is an ongoing process that continues long after the deliverance session.

THE PROCESS OF FORGIVENESS

Unforgiveness is a primary piece of garbage that opens the door for demonic invasion. Some Christians do not understand forgiveness. Once, I was ministering to a Christian brother who was contemplating divorce. As I prayed over him, nothing came out. However, I heard the Holy Spirit say, "Unforgiveness. His parents." I stopped the prayer and asked the young man about it.

"No," he said, "I forgave my parents a long time ago."

The following week, he came back for more prayer. Once again, the Holy Spirit said, "Unforgiveness. His parents." I asked him again.

He repeated his confident answer, "I forgave them a long time ago."

I switched the subject to ancestral curses and asked him what he knew about his ancestors.

"Nothing," he replied.

"Maybe you should talk to your parents," I remarked. "Ask them what they know about your ancestors."

"No way," he said, "I forgave them, but I don't have to talk to them. I stopped talking to them ten years ago."

His parents lived only a few blocks from him, yet they hadn't spoken with each other in a decade.

Genuine forgiveness restores relationships wherever possible or practicable. Certainly, there are cases where it may not be healthy or prudent to restore a relationship, as in cases with a history of abuse or assault, but such circumstances are rare. For the most part, when it comes to hurts from family and friends, restoring a relationship with them not only brings spiritual and emotional healing but also stands as a reminder of God's forgiveness toward each one of us.

Love is the basis of forgiveness; love seeks to restore relationships. God does not want resentment and bitterness to take root in your heart. In truth, a person can forgive somebody yet still harbor bitterness against him or her.

Some believers see forgiveness as simply issuing a blanket statement: "I forgive everyone in the whole wide world who has ever sinned against me from the time I was born until now." Unfortunately, it is not that easy. God requires forgiveness of specific people for specific actions before demonic bondages can be broken. That is, one should mention the person's name and forgive the specific trespass he or she committed.

Forgiveness is like an onion that is peeled in layers. When I was young, someone hurt me over a length of time. Before I became a Christian, I would engage in long discussions about all the hurts that person gave me. After becoming a Christian, I forgave that individual, but I would still occasionally participate in "poor me" sessions where the hurts were reopened and examined. My wife would say, "I thought you forgave that person." I would stop in my tracks and think, *I guess I haven't.* Then I would forgive again. A few months later, the hurts would come up again, although maybe not as intense as before. My wife would say once more, "I thought you forgave." Once again, I would go through the process of forgiving that person. Finally, after three or four cycles of repenting and forgiving, I eventually stopped complaining about the person altogether—not because I consciously disciplined myself, but because it just never came up. I had finally completed the forgiveness process.

> Unforgiveness is a primary piece of garbage that opens the door for demonic invasion.

As a rule, the deeper the hurt, the deeper the forgiveness has to go. In some cases, it will take more than one attempt at forgiveness. I'm not saying that people cannot forgive something in one sitting; in some cases, they can. However, since demons attach to deep-seated resentments, if forgiveness becomes a process, deliverance will also become a process.

DEALING WITH EMOTIONS AND HABITS

Often, one needs to deal with personal problems and habits before deliverance can bring about permanent improvement. This is especially true when the person has other emotional or psychological problems. In such cases, there is usually no quick, Band-Aid treatment.

I recall a woman who had been in psychiatric sessions to treat paranoia for more than twelve years. After one session with me, she never came back, complaining that she did not receive complete healing. Although anything is possible with God, you cannot expect long-standing emotional issues to be completely cured in one session without miraculous, divine intervention. It takes time to deal with personalities, habits, compulsions, and emotions. If these issues are not accurately identified and fully addressed, the smiles and alleluias immediately after deliverance will soon be followed by a return to the same old depression, fears, and emotions experienced before.

Rejection

People dealing with the pain of rejection tend to see the world through the tinted lenses of rejection. They will often interpret innocent body postures and words as personal slights and will walk away angry and insulted. They may interpret an innocent gaze on your part as judgment and scorn. Nothing you say or do will convince them otherwise. Dealing with these attitudes can become daily events, even after deliverance.

Some people who have experienced deep rejection develop dysfunctional or immature personalities. Something triggers them, and no matter how great the relationship was before, they suddenly withdraw, convinced that they have been slighted in some way. Such people covet love but are frustrated because it seems they can never get enough.

Dealing with the Garbage

Somehow, they have to fight through their long-established reactions. In most cases, other people in their lives have either disappeared or are simply ignoring the inappropriate behavior because it is too difficult to deal with directly. The best thing to do is to sit them down and point out their specific social or personal dysfunctional behavior. If you can get them to agree to allow you, as a friend, to point out such actions as they occur, it can pave the way to improvement.

One rejected person constantly burped at the dinner table and never thought anything about it. When I pointed it out to him, he left to pout in his room. Earlier, he had stated that he never had a mother or father to teach him about manners and proper behavior in public. However, every time I tried to correct him, he was offended. He began to change when I pointed out what the Bible says:

"For whom the LORD loves He chastens, and scourges every son whom He receives." If you endure chastening, God deals with you as with sons; for what son is there whom a father does not chasten? But if you are without chastening, of which all have become partakers, then you are illegitimate and not sons. (Hebrews 12:6–8)

In addition,

Open rebuke is better than love carefully concealed. Faithful are the wounds of a friend, but the kisses of an enemy are deceitful. (Proverbs 27:5–6)

Your best friend is the person who rebukes and corrects you so that you will become a better person. Your worst enemy is the one who makes you think that you are fine when you are actually inadequate.

It is essential for those suffering from rejection to be willing to accept rebuke and correction from those whom they trust. If they don't, they will never change. Real life change will only happen through a conscious decision to be transformed through constant exposure to the Word of God.

Rejected people are self-oriented and not God-oriented; they do not have the welfare of the group or church at heart. They will abandon the church or leader if offended for any reason. They are not likely to serve the Lord for long. Every true servant of God must deal with rejection because it is inevitable if one is a follower of Jesus.

> Rejected people are self-oriented and not God-oriented; they do not have the welfare of the group or church at heart.

Prophets in particular cannot truly serve God well if they have a rejected person's attitudes and fear him or her. What if a pastor of a large church invites you to speak at his church and he is known to give a generous love offering? He puts you up in a beautiful hotel, sends you a fruit basket, and provides a limousine to pick you up.

Then, as you walk to the podium, God speaks to you: "Tell this pastor right now that if he does not stop doing what he is doing and repent before Me, I am going to remove him!" Will you speak the word as God gave it to you or will you water it down? Will you say, "God loves you very much, but I feel that He wants you to think about what you are doing and if it is not good, to quit doing it"? Will you care more about pleasing God than pleasing man?

Dealing with the Garbage

I have a very good friend who is a true prophet of God. He and his wife came from out of town to visit me one day. We were sitting down at dinner when I told my friend, "I believe that you are a prophet of God, but that means you need to get rid of your rejected spirit, because you will have a hard time if you are afraid of rejection." When I said that, my friend stood up—all six feet four inches of him—walked behind me, and gave me a big bear hug! He wept and said to me, "You don't know how much you have blessed me!"

His wife added, "He hasn't prophesied for over two years. God hasn't spoken to him. He has been praying and crying out to God and still God hasn't talked to him and he cannot prophesy. He used to be tall and real skinny for his age and all the kids used to tease him and call him 'stork,' and he never got over it."

I prayed for him right there in the restaurant. Two days later, he prophesied for the first time in over two years.

It is important for a rejected person to learn to accept the love of God as well as to begin to give love to God and to others. If you are not a loving person, you will go around looking for love but will not be able to find it; but if love is who you are, no matter where you are, love is there.

"There is no fear in love; but perfect love casts out fear" (1 John 4:18). The seed of rejection is fear. Fortunately for us, love always conquers fear.

ONGOING SIN

Ongoing sin is another pile of garbage that attracts flies. Some believers ask for deliverance in one area while they are harboring hidden sin in another area. For instance, a man may desire deliverance from fear but is engaging in premarital sex with his girlfriend. In such an instance, deliverance will not work. God is not in the habit of blessing people who are openly and freely sinning. Until there is true repentance, which includes a turning from the sinful practice, permanent relief is not possible.

I am a firm believer that God wants to heal and deliver everyone. So, why does God heal someone with a bad heart and yet not heal the person standing next to him with an identical ailment?

Once, I prayed for two women standing side by side who both had heart problems. One was healed instantly, and the other was not. Why does such a thing happen? My guess would be that there were most likely existing curses or rights that the enemy had in the person who did not receive healing. The same thing is true with deliverance.

On one of my visits to Baguio, in the Philippines, a woman came to me for deliverance. She said, in almost a bragging way, "Nobody can deliver me. I've been prayed over by many people from America, and no one can get my demons out."

I asked her the usual questions about unforgiveness and ongoing sins. She denied both. I assigned a team of workers who commanded demons to leave her for almost forty-five minutes and the demons refused to come out.

"Are you sure there is no barrier to deliverance, like ongoing sins?" I asked.

"Absolutely sure!" was the confident answer.

Two days later, the concierge at the front desk of my hotel called me downstairs because someone wanted to speak with me. I went down to the lobby and saw that the same woman was waiting for me with her American husband. She quickly approached and asked me a question.

"I heard that you are an attorney from America," the woman said. "Can we ask you a legal question?"

"Sure," I replied.

She said, "My husband and I have been living together for eleven years and we have two children. He originally lived in California, where he had a wife and three children. They were separated for over twelve years. Do you think he needs to get a legal divorce?"

This woman and her husband had no concept of sin. Many Christians do not understand repentance either. I have heard longtime Christians pray like this: "Dear Lord, I repent of all the sins I ever committed since I was born," or, "Dear God, I repent of all the sins I have committed against my wife."

> As long as you live in a fleshly body, you must work continually to renew your mind to keep improper thoughts and attitudes in check.

Just as with forgiveness, we need to get specific about our sin is if we want deliverance from demons that cling to specific sins. Of course, such repentance has to be genuine.

EVIL THOUGHTS AND ATTITUDES

You do not wash a pig and then return it to its muddy sty. In the same way, it is necessary to renew the mind even after demons have left.

For I delight in the law of God according to the inward man. But I see another law in my members, warring against the law of my mind, and bringing me into captivity to the law of sin which is in my members....So then, with the mind I myself serve the law of God, but with the flesh the law of sin. (Romans 7:22-23, 25)

Here, the apostle Paul revealed that there is a law of sin in the flesh. Even if you have no demons in you, you still have to deal with the sin nature of your flesh. Additionally, Paul stated, *"But I discipline my body and bring it into subjection, lest, when I have preached to others, I myself should become disqualified"* (1 Corinthians 9:27). Demons or no demons, even the great apostle Paul had to keep his body under subjection. As long as you live in a fleshly body, you must work continually to renew your mind to keep improper thoughts and attitudes in check.

James wrote, *"Therefore lay aside all filthiness and overflow of wickedness, and receive with meekness the implanted word, which is able to save your souls"* (James 1:21). In this passage, he was not talking to unbelievers; he was addressing the followers of Jesus Christ. He recognized that many Christians had formerly led decrepit lives and had to change their ways of thinking and attitudes in many areas. The word *soul* refers to the mind, intellect, will, and emotions.

We need to lay aside our evil thoughts of selfishness and rebellion and filter our thoughts, habits, and attitudes through the Word of God. Humankind, in the natural, is selfish, self-centered, and not apt to love others unless there is some direct benefit. *"All our righteousnesses are like filthy rags"* (Isaiah 64:6). Scripture reminds us that our best ideas and concepts of good are *"like filthy rags"* to God. Only one standard will lead us to a renewed mind and holiness. It is the Word of God. Therefore, encourage daily reading of the Bible in order to implant the Word of God firmly into the heart and mind. Then, encourage obedience to the Word in every situation.

One can assent intellectually to the truths in the Bible and yet not live them out. A determination to live in truth and spirit will go a long way to permanent healing.

Some believers will gossip, complain, backstab, exhibit jealousy and envy, and do many things that suggest that the door is still open for demonic invasion in their life. Wrath, strife, sedition, and other rebellious attitudes can clearly indicate that the person being counseled has not yet filled the voids in his or her life with the fruit of the Spirit. He or she is yet carnal.

> *Now the works of the flesh are evident, which are: adultery, fornication, uncleanness, lewdness, idolatry, sorcery, hatred, contentions, jealousies, outbursts of wrath, selfish ambitions, dissensions, heresies, envy, murders, drunkenness, revelries, and the like; of which I tell you beforehand, just as I also told you in time past, that those who practice such things will not inherit the kingdom of God.*
>
> (Galatians 5:19–21)

Deliverance without a permanent change in attitude can reopen the door for spirits of rebellion and pride. Holiness is the most effective way to keep demons out. Jesus said, *"The ruler of this world is coming, and he has nothing in Me"* (John 14:30). There was no open door, no back door, and no garbage—nothing in Jesus for Satan to gain a foothold. Sadly, such an emphasis on holiness is rarely preached or taught in churches today.

CHAPTER TWO

DELIVERANCE AND INNER HEALING

Inner healing is a method of dealing with the negative emotions and mind-sets within a person that shape his or her outward behavior. They tend to take the form of wrong conclusions, negative agreements, and bad attitudes. In my opinion, these inner realities of the mind and soul are as much a part of spiritual warfare as are the deliberate attacks of demons that must be cast out.

The subject of inner healing has been a controversial issue among Christians. There are some who believe that inner healing is too close to secular psychiatry or occult techniques. I am similarly concerned about occult techniques and shy away from anything that smacks of the occult. On the other hand, I also realize that not everything done in the secular world is the exclusive property of the devil. Remember, the devil has never created anything; he can only counterfeit and corrupt the legitimate creations of God. The structure and functions of the mind all stem from the blueprint of God's original creation.

Others believe that inner healing deals too much with the mind and soul, and not enough with the spirit. However, the mind and soul of man are as much the gifts of God as is the spirit. As long as we look to the Holy Spirit in us as our primary source of understanding and power, and our direct link to God, we can avoid trouble.

Of course, there are times when certain cases are better left to professional Christian counselors or psychiatrists, especially when people have been professionally diagnosed as being schizophrenic, bipolar, or having other mental or emotional disease.

There are many instances, however, where a little knowledge of Christian inner healing can go a long way in setting the captives free. The intent of this chapter is to help ordinary Christians be prepared to love and nurture the brokenhearted or bruised individual. For this purpose, I will document several actual cases in order to give a better understanding for what is being discussed.

SATAN'S BATTLEGROUND: THE MIND

Satan's primary weapons are deception and lies, and his primary stronghold is the mind. As Paul said in 2 Corinthians 10:4–5:

(For the weapons of our warfare are not carnal, but mighty through God to the pulling down of strong holds;) casting down imaginations, and every high thing that exalteth itself against the knowledge of God, and bringing into captivity every thought to the obedience of Christ. (KJV)

How do you cast down imaginations? What are imaginations made of? In my experience, they tend to be made up of such things as wrong conclusions, negative agreements, and bad attitudes. Such mind-sets exalt themselves against *"the knowledge of God"* and His ways. In Scripture, we are commanded to bring into captivity every thought to the obedience of Christ. Hence, as these imaginations are exposed, we are to cast them down.

Inner healing, including the healing of memories, is closely associated to deliverance and constitutes a crucial way of casting down such ungodly attitudes and thought patterns. Often, these are not simply human weaknesses of the flesh but result from demonic activity and direct spiritual attack. Frequently, as God cleanses and heals such hurtful memories, inner healing will work hand-in-hand with deliverance, and the demons will flee automatically.

> As God cleanses and heals hurtful memories, inner healing will work hand-in-hand with deliverance, and the demons will flee.

The Bible tells us that at least a portion of the battleground is in the mind: *"Do not be conformed to this world, but be transformed by the renewing of your mind, that you may prove what is that good and acceptable and perfect will of God"* (Romans 12:2).

James added: *"Therefore lay aside all filthiness and overflow of wickedness, and receive with meekness the implanted word, which is able to save your souls. But be doers of the word, and not hearers only, deceiving yourselves"* (James 1:21–22). It is the Word of God that can renew our minds. However, we are not only to read and hear the Word; we are also to do it!

Certainly, there are times when deliverance alone is the right application. There may be other times when inner healing alone is needed. Sometimes it will take both, and sometimes neither. It takes wisdom, experience, and discernment to know what to apply and when.[2]

The Effect of Lies

In my earlier book, *Spiritual Warfare*, I stated that Satan and his evil spirits cannot enter into the bodies of people without a legal right, and such rights usually take the form of curses. Since then, my experience in this matter has only served to further confirm that statement. Evil spirits can readily enter the body and affect the mind if that person agrees with the lies of the enemy. However, once such lies are renounced, the demons have no right to stay. Very often, as soon as the lie is renounced, the demons leave without much effort at all on the part of the counselor.

A Case History

In Fiji, a woman around fifty years of age once related that she had a difficult time trusting people, especially men. She stated that her husband was a sweet Christian man, but she could not love him. She did not want to deprive him of intimacy, but she had no feelings or desire when it came to sex.

I asked the Holy Spirit to show us what happened in her past to bring about this situation. Immediately, she recalled a time when she was fourteen and her stepfather was sexually abusing her.

As she wept, I asked her, "Because of this, what has the devil told you?"

Deliverance and Inner Healing

She answered, "Don't trust men. Sex is dirty. All men are filthy. Don't let them touch you!" She continued to weep.

I reminded her that Jesus is a man, and that if she could trust Jesus then perhaps there *were* men that could be trusted. She nodded and renounced the lies aloud.

Immediately she fell to her knees and coughed and vomited for almost five minutes. All I did was observe what was going on. I didn't say a word and did not lay hands on her. God was working. The demons were fleeing because a lie had been replaced by the truth.

Later, as the coughing started to slow down, I called out the spirits of fear, rejection, shame, embarrassment, distrust, and all related spirits. Once again, she went into a coughing spell. In the end, she smiled and felt tremendous release.

DESTROYING THE ENEMY'S RIGHTS

Renouncing the lies of Satan not only heals the mind by destroying false attitudes, it also takes away the right of the enemy to stay. Apparently, lies open the door for demonic activity to enter, while truth shuts the door and keeps them out. Inner healing involves not only the cleansing of bad memories and wrong attitudes, but also the casting out of demons that come in with the lies.

Scripture clearly states that we are to pursue truth: "*You desire truth in the inward parts*" (Psalm 51:6). Likewise, Scripture states that "*Jesus is the way, the truth, and the life*" (John 14:6), and that the Holy Spirit is "*the Spirit of truth*" (John 14:17, 16:13). When Ananias and Sapphira lied to the Holy Spirit, they died. (See Acts 5:1–10.) When the church saw this, they experienced a great time of unity and power as the apostles did tremendous signs and wonders and many were added to their numbers. (See Acts 5:11–16.) There is an inherent power in truth, as there is in lies.

God's kingdom is the kingdom of truth; Satan's realm is the realm of lies and deceit. Satan strives to establish lies in the minds of humans everywhere. Jesus said that Satan is the father of lies. (See John 8:44.) Through lies, Satan can gain at least partial—and sometimes complete—control of the minds of men and women. In the end times, Satan will attempt to control the entire world through means of deception. (See Revelation 12:9 and 13:14.)

LIES BIND US TO THE PAST

Some lies and hurtful memories may be so deeply entrenched that we are unaware of the effect they have on our current attitudes and behavior. We may struggle to change, but to no avail. Forgetting the past and moving on with God is an impossible dream for many bruised in their past. After a while, many Christians despair of ever changing and simply give up. Little do they realize that their past has them in chains. Everyone has a past, but when the past has you, you are in trouble.

Even if they do have a vivid memory of what happened in their past, most people do not know how to wipe out the negative effects of those events. It is often more than a matter of forgiveness. For some, their emotions are like a roller coaster, tossing them up and down. One day there is depression, the next there is delight, only to be followed by another dive into the valley of despair the following day. Mood changes, fear, crying, and moaning are always lurking around the corner. They have tried counseling, prayer, fasting, and all kinds of advice. Nothing works. There seems to be no relief in sight. Jesus said,

> *The Spirit of the Lord is upon me, because he hath anointed me to preach the gospel to the poor; he hath sent me to heal the brokenhearted, to preach deliverance to the captives, and recovering of sight to the blind, to set at liberty them that are bruised.* (Luke 4:18 KJV)

In that passage, I see the *"brokenhearted"* frequently as the victims or rape or physical abuse. They can also be the children of divorce and broken families or the casualties of neglect and rejection. The *"bruised"* may be those who still suffer from deep hurts and wounds that never heal and continue to haunt them throughout life. It is the boy whose alcoholic father beat him daily; the girl abandoned to foster parents; the child who found his mother hanging in the closet; or the youngster molested by a sexual deviant.

MECHANICS OF THE HUMAN MIND

In order to understand inner healing and to move in cooperation with the Holy Spirit, it helps to understand the mechanics of the human mind. Perhaps the manner by which the mind works will shed light on why we do certain things so we can understand the process of inner healing.

For the sake of our discussion, the human mind has three major parts:

1) the unconscious—where the all the memories of life's experiences are stored;

2) the subconscious—where the decisions, beliefs, and mind-sets brought about by life's experiences are stored;

3) the conscious—where one acts and responds to the physical world around him or her.

Imagine a triangle divided into three compartments. At the bottom is a large base, taking up at least four-fifths of the triangle. This is the unconscious mind, where all our memories are stored. In the middle is the subconscious mind, where our attitudes and beliefs are stored. At the very top, the smallest area is the conscious mind, by which we respond to the world around us.

The mind stores up bits of information, even when you are asleep. It retains physical facts such as the scenery where events happened—a room and its contents, who was there, the time, the weather, the temperature, and who was doing what. It also logs conversations, the emotions experienced, the smells, noises, even tastes and physical feelings or sensations. The mind stores up everything, even things that happened when you were in your mother's womb.

Dr. Wilder Penfield (1891–1976), a noted Canadian neurosurgeon who pioneered techniques to treat epilepsy, published accounts of amazing and vivid memory recall when certain temporal lobes of the central cortex of the brain were stimulated with a low electrical current.[3] The fully conscious patients not only recalled events, but also smelled the odors, tasted the food, felt the emotions, and knew the thoughts that took place at the time of the incident. The study supported the idea that our brains not only store memories of each event but also retain all the physical details as well as the senses that were aroused or that responded to the incident when it took place.

In one of Dr. Penfield's studies, a woman in her fifties immediately recalled standing in a baby crib as an infant. She was about one year old at the time. She could smell an apple pie baking in the oven and hear her aunt playing a song on the piano. As she recalled the memory, she actually recited the words and lyrics played. She had a feeling of great well-being. Yet, in her conscious mind, she had no memory of the event or the song.

The obvious conclusion is that all of the events of our lives, good or bad, are stored up in the unconscious portion of our mind.

Extra Emphasis Given to Traumatic Events

While the mind stores all experiences, it seems to give priority or elevated status to certain traumatic or life-threatening events. In other words, the mind puts an emphasis on events that jeopardized a person's life or that of a loved one. Our brains are designed for survival and will place an emphasis on such dramatic instances. It is actually a defense mechanism. The threat of bodily harm, and our subsequent survival of it, teaches us to avoid or repel such danger in the future.

All of the events of our lives, good or bad, are stored up in the unconscious portion of our mind.

For instance, if a child sticks his hand into a burning fire he feels immediate pain and pulls his hand back instinctively. His brain instantly concludes that if he sticks his hand into a fire in the future, he will feel pain and it will pose a threat to his well-being. He stores the thought: *Fires burn and hurt.*

Do not stick your hand into a fire. Thereafter, whenever he sees a fire, the brain is automatically stimulated and the memory comes to the forefront—perhaps not as a unified thought, but as a need to avoid pain.

To a large extent, the brain's function in this area is a positive function. It helps us to survive. However, we can also develop and store wrong conclusions, beliefs, thoughts, and attitudes in the same manner.

A CASE STUDY

In one case, a professional hula dancer related that she had to overcome tremendous stage fright each time she performed. Her life was miserable and she was in danger of losing her job. She often had an upset stomach and wanted to vomit backstage. Whenever she danced before an audience, she had to mentally block out the audience and make believe that no one was there watching her.

We asked God to show her what happened in her past to make her so afraid to perform in front of people. Almost immediately, God took her all the way back to her days in kindergarten. She remembered one day when she wanted to use the restroom but was shy and afraid to ask the teacher, so she wet her pants. When the teacher found out, she dragged the girl before the entire class and had all the youngsters point at her and laugh. Ever since that humiliating and hurtful experience, she had developed a fear of having groups of people staring at her.

"What did you conclude at the time?" I asked her.

"When you stand in front of people," she replied, "they will reject you, make fun of you, and make you feel ashamed of yourself."

Deliverance and Inner Healing

As we renounced the lies of the enemy, the memory faded away. A week later she happily reported that the stage fright had disappeared when she performed.

PAINFUL MEMORIES

As previously noted, negative memories are usually born out of traumatic experiences or losses. At one end of the spectrum of traumatic experiences is a near-death experience or the threat of dire physical injury or distress. It could be a rape, sexual molestation, physical abuse, an automobile accident, or some other life-threatening event. Loss could be the death of a family member, pet, friend, or something closely identified with the person. It could also be the loss of property, such as the family home burning down or the destruction of a prized possession such as a car or family business. Whenever we suffer loss, we experience feelings of sadness, grief, resentment, hurt, and even anger. These emotions may cling to us.

Interestingly, at the other end of the spectrum is rejection, often heavy but sometimes slight—real or imagined—which is also perceived by the mind as life-threatening, trauma-producing, or threatening to our well-being. This can include episodes of embarrassment, shame, sexual or verbal abuse, and the like. Rejection by a mother, even an inadvertent rejection in the early days soon after birth, can be interpreted as life-threatening from an infant's viewpoint.

A CASE HISTORY

A woman once came to me with fears of abandonment and loneliness. It turned out that when she was five years old her mother took her to a sale at a department store. The child became lost in the frenzy and cried for her mother. Eventually she was taken to the lost and found, where they fed her ice cream to soothe her fears. When her mother came to retrieve her, the child was calm and smiling. However, somewhere during that event the devil told her that her mother did not love her; that she would be abandoned, lonely, and unloved the rest of her life. Subconsciously, she agreed with those lies. From that time on, the woman suffered from acute shyness, loneliness, distrust, and a fear of abandonment.

WHAT MAKES UP AN EXPERIENCE?

The brain stores up every event of life. As explained above, many things besides physical experiences or scenes make up an experience. The mind also stores up emotions and physical feelings such as pain, body postures, or decisions connected with the experience. Such emotions are also manifested in the physical body—fast heartbeat, tightening of neck muscles, clenching of fists, or flushing in the face. These physical reactions are stored as well.

The mind may store up nonsensical or disconnected items such as a bird that flew by just seconds before an accident, a pair of fuzzy dice hanging from a rearview mirror, or an ashtray on the table just before the stove blew up. In the future, this may lead to a fear of birds. An ashtray may become a forbidden item in the house for no logical or apparent reason. Seeing a pair of dice may trigger unexplained feelings of anxiety.

The human brain is incredible. It stores up all the events of our life, often in vivid detail. Most of the time, however, we do not have the conscious ability to recall them from our memory banks. The incidents are too old to remember, or our mind suppresses the memory along with the hurt in order to help us cope on the conscious level and go on with life. Out of nowhere, these stored nuggets can surface because of current experience that serve as triggers.

SOME TRIGGERS

A masseur in my church related that his clients often recalled traumatic events of the past as he massaged certain sore areas of their bodies. One woman had a deep fear of the ocean. As he massaged a tight spot on her back, she began to weep as she recalled that her younger brother drowned many years ago, and she immediately recognized the source of her fear. At other times, memories of auto accidents or the death of a loved one would resurface, and the person was able to release the latent emotions that originally accompanied the experience.

BODY SENSATIONS OR POSTURES

We may feel a pain in our right knee, which we do not associate with any particular incident, but it is material to the memory recall. As we concentrate on the pain, the entire memory may unfold. Sometimes, we experience it as a tingling or cold spot. At other times, it is warmth, tightness, pain, or other physical feeling. These sensations are part of the total experience and can conjure up the rest of the memory. Up to this point, however, the mere remembrance or recall of an experience is merely a physiological process, not a spiritual event.

Sometimes, I ask the subject to concentrate on some negative emotion such as fear or anger, and I ask him or her to look for some kind of bodily sensation. If he or she is able to locate a somewhat unusual pain, coldness, warmth, tingling, or other physical feeling, I ask him to concentrate on that spot; very often, the memory starts to unfold.

At other times, however, the person is simply unable to recall a particular event. In such cases, only the Holy Spirit can unlock the source of the problem and bring forth to the conscious memory the early experience that gave rise to the particular mind-set, mood, or emotion causing personal difficulties in the present.

NEGATIVE AGREEMENTS

Not all current responses derive from traumatic events relating to survival. We learn many of our fear responses through agreements with others or ourselves. I was once at a party where a huge cockroach started crawling up the dining room wall. Some of the women screamed, and most of the men jumped back, trying to act brave but with pounding hearts. A tiny woman on the side exclaimed, "Oh, you dirty, little thing!" She just walked over to the crawling cockroach and grabbed it with her bare hand. She flushed it down the toilet. She had absolutely no fear in her eyes. Yet, I have seen grown men paralyzed in terror by the site of a cockroach.

> In many cases, only the Holy Spirit can unlock the source of the problem causing personal difficulties in the present.

Some people are terrified by gecko lizards; others love to play with them. I love geckos. When I was young, I would grab them with my bare hands and stick them in my side pocket so I could bring them to school. Roaches, on the other hand, terrify me. Somewhere inside of me, I made an agreement with myself that geckos were harmless, but roaches were to be feared. My wife made an opposite agreement. She is terrified of lizards, yet unaffected by roaches.

Much of our attitudes about ourselves stem from some sort of negative agreement in our past. Often these sprout from negative statements that we, as parents, give to our children: "You're so clumsy," "You're stupid!"; "You'll never amount to anything!"; "How'd you get so ugly?"

A young mind will accept just about anything as truth when it comes from someone older or in a position of authority. If the mind forms an agreement with the statement, from that point all the resources of the mind will be used to defend and support that negative agreement. Such agreements do not necessarily distinguish between something that is "good" or "bad."

> If the mind forms an agreement with a negative statement, from that point all the resources of the mind will be used to defend and support that agreement.

When my oldest son was in elementary school, he was a terrible student, and all of his test scores were below average. His teachers would console me by saying, "Well, not everybody is born smart. Anyway, he's a nice boy." I, however, told him repeatedly that he was a smart boy. I reminded him that while girls tend to be intellectually ahead of boys early in life, studies show that boys tend to catch up with the girls by high school and college.

When he was in the eighth grade, he began to attain a few As for the first time. His grade point average was 3.65 the last three years in high school. In college, he graduated with honors and had a grade point average of 4.0 his last two years, having achieved an average of 3.8 in his major. He became a member of the National Honor Society and received a scholarship for three years of law school. The power of agreement can work both ways.

CHAPTER THREE

REVERSING NEGATIVE AGREEMENTS

If we can get people to recall those long-buried traumatic events and discern the negative agreements (those bringing about unacceptable or destructive behavior) they entered into as a result, then through the power of the Holy Spirit, we can neutralize those agreements and free them from both physical and psychological oppression. Likewise, if we can lead people in making positive statements of affirmation that they can agree with, it can change their behavior.

All this may sound a bit like reprogramming a computer. It is, in a sense. However, it does not mean that we can automatically change a person's attitude and mind-set by throwing a switch or clicking a button as with a computer. After all, humans have the fluctuations of will, intellect, and emotion that a computer does not.

I am well aware that governments and other institutions have shamefully used principles like these to brainwash entire groups of people. In truth, these methods can be used for good or for evil. Our aim, however, is not to manipulate minds for our own gain or purpose. Our intent is to help individuals with the destructive problems that keep repeating in their lives—problems caused by negative agreements, attitudes, and conclusions.

In order to heal these "bruises of the mind and heart," we first need to uncover the memories or incidents that are the underlying source of the problem. Second, we need to uncover the negative agreements or lies created by the experience. Third, we need to renounce those lies or negative agreements and substitute an opposite, positive agreement in their place.

A CASE STUDY

Twenty-year-old Susan came into my office two weeks before Christmas. She explained how the holidays were the worst time of the year for her. Ever since she could remember, she had been sick every Christmas.

I asked her to close her eyes, and we prayed together, asking God to show her what happened when she was young to cause this problem. She concentrated on being sick at Christmas. Instantly, Susan recalled a scene when she was five or six years old. She was at home in her living room, where there was a Christmas tree. Everyone was scurrying around, preparing for a party that evening. In their rush, they forgot to feed Susan lunch. She felt neglected and started sobbing. Still, no one noticed her. Finally, she started to cry louder and ended up vomiting. Her parents and aunt ran to her and hugged her. "Oh, Mommy is so sorry, we forgot to feed you." They prepared her a great lunch, including ice cream. Her father took her riding in his new Buick in hopes that the wind would make her feel better. Susan was delighted.

I asked her, "What did you decide then, Susan?"

After a little prodding, Susan said, "It's good to get sick. Then everybody will love you."

Every year, like clockwork, the smells and sights of Christmas all became triggers that brought on Susan's sickness.

First, I had Susan renounce that lie: "I renounce the lie that I have to get sick for people to love me. It is not true."

I then had her affirm the truth: "I do not have to get sick for people to love me. People love me all the time. I deserve to be loved, and I am capable of loving others."

We asked the Lord to erase the memories and take them away. I had Susan open her eyes and then close them after a minute.

> When counseling people, always try to go beyond the incident to identify and confront the lie that was formed.

"Susan, please go back to that memory and tell me what you see." Now, the memory had begun to fade away, and Susan had a hard time remembering it. In the end, it was gone.

The first week of January, she called me. "Guess what?" she said. "I didn't get sick during Christmas for the first time since I was young." The smells and emotions no longer triggered a sick response. God had set Susan free.

This is a classic example of dealing with negative agreements:

1) recall the memory or incident (neglected at Christmas);

2) expose the negative agreement or lie ("If I get sick, people will love me");

3) renounce the lie and replace it with a truth ("I don't have to get sick for people to love me").

Most of the time, but not always, a traumatic experience before adulthood, most likely between the ages of one and ten, can give rise to these incorrect attitudes and agreements. Although some of these experiences can be traumatic, such as a car accident or physical abuse, others can be something simple, like missing lunch or hearing an off-hand comment. Don't allow yourself to judge the severity of the incident; the incident doesn't matter. We are trying to get at the negative agreements they caused.

When counseling people, always try to go beyond the incident to identify and confront the lie that was formed. Then have the counselee renounce it and affirm the truth when it is appropriate.

REPETITIVE PROBLEMS WITH RELATIONSHIPS

Sometimes people experience destructive problems in their relationships with other people. Unexplained emotions and actions arise out of nowhere to sabotage friendships, courtship, and even marriages. Often, the cause is a traumatic past experience that led to a negative agreement with the self.

Reversing Negative Agreements

A CASE STUDY

Jan came into my office with a boy she introduced as her boyfriend, Herman. He was a nice-looking young man, and they made the "perfect couple." Jan was a very attractive twenty-year-old with red hair and green eyes. Two weeks later, she came to my office with tears in her eyes. She had just broken up with her boyfriend.

I tried to console her: "Well, Jan, you're attractive. You'll find another boyfriend."

"But that's the seventh boyfriend I've had in the last two years."

"Wow, Jan, that's really moving fast."

"But you don't understand. Every time a boy tells me that he is falling in love with me or I sense that he is, I cannot stand him anymore. I actually hate him and do not want him around me. When Herman told me that he was falling for me, I yelled, 'Who told you to fall for me?' Then I hung up the phone on him."

"Jan," I said, "I want you to close your eyes and pray with me: 'Dear Jesus, I thank You so much for Your love and Your faithfulness. I ask You, Lord, to help me recall the incident and bring to my memory anything that may have happened in my past that would cause me to reject the love of others. Holy Spirit, please come and help me recall what happened.'"

At this point, I tried to help Jan recall the incident by asking a few questions. When doing this, try to be direct and authoritative, more or less demanding a person's mind to recall the event. This is to ensure that the mind does not become comfortable and resort back to covering up the unpleasant memory.

"Jan," I asked, "what do you see? Where are you?"

"In my bedroom. It's dark."

"Who is there with you?"

"My sister."

"How old are you?"

"About nine years old."

"How old is your sister?"

"About seven years old."

"What is happening?"

"I'm sitting up in bed talking to my sister."

"What are you saying?"

"I hate you! If a robber came into the house and said he would let everyone go but he had to kill someone, I would tell him to kill you!"

"How do you feel?"

"I hate her. I wish she were dead."

"What happened next?"

Jan paused.

"My sister died three months later," she said.

"Open your eyes, Jan," I said. "Now tell me, what happened to your sister?"

"She had leukemia. My parents knew but never told me. All I knew was that they gave her everything, but they ignored me. I didn't know."

"When did you find out?"

"Not until I was fourteen."

Reversing Negative Agreements

"Did you kill your sister, Jan?"

"No, but for years I thought I did."

I then asked her to close her eyes. "Jan, what decision did you make when she died?"

She thought about it for a minute or so. Then she said, "I'm a murderer! I don't deserve to be loved. If anyone gets close to me, they will find out how horrible I am. They will learn my secret that I killed my sister."

"Jan," I said, "that's a lie. You didn't kill your sister."

"I know."

"Jan, let's reverse that lie. Please repeat after me: 'Dear God, thank You so much for bringing that memory back to me. In the name of Jesus Christ, I rebuke Satan for putting a lie in my mind. I am not a murderer. I did not kill my sister. I loved her. I deserve to be loved, and I am capable of loving others. When people get to know me, they will find that I am a fine person, full of love and kindness. I love my sister and my parents, and I forgive my parents for what happened.'"

I then asked Jan to reconstruct the memory, but this time I asked Jan to hug her sister and tell her how much she loved her. I had Jan tell her sister that she was glad she was with Jesus and that, one day, they would be together forever. We closed by praying as follows:

Dear Jesus, thank You once again for Your love and faithfulness. Please heal the wounds in Jan's heart and in her mind. Fill up the void places with Your love, Your Word, and Your Holy Spirit. Let Jan know the depth of Your love for her and that she has been found worthy by Your blood. Thank You Lord. Amen.

The last I heard, Jan was happily married.

A CASE STUDY

Laurie came to see me about a petition for divorce that her husband had filed against her. The state in which she lived was a "no-fault" state and there were no defenses.

"Laurie," I told her, "as you know, we cannot stop this petition. However, I want to help rehabilitate you so that you will not repeat whatever is behind this divorce. I want you to think about your responsibility in the matter."

Laurie became irate. "What do you mean my responsibility? He's the one who has a girlfriend. I'm not the one who cheated."

"Okay, all I ask is that you go home and think it over. We'll talk about this again next week."

A week later, Laurie was more contrite.

"I apologize, Mr. Ing. When I went home, I began to think about what you said. My husband was really a nice person when I married him. He did all the shopping and cooking, helped with the dishes, and cleaned the house all the time. However, when we used to watch TV at night I could not stand to have him sit next to me. I used to tell him to sit elsewhere. I don't know why. After a while, I didn't want him around so I suggested that he take up bowling. Then I told him that he should go more often. Eventually, he was out bowling four nights a week."

Laurie paused at this point and tears came to her eyes as she continued: "That's where he met his girlfriend. She even called me one day and asked me if I was sure that I wanted to let my husband go. She said she didn't know why some wouldn't want to date such a nice guy."

"What did you tell her?"

"I told her she could have him."

Laurie then added, "He really *is* a nice guy, and I don't know why I didn't want him around."

"Laurie, do you want to find out why?"

She nodded, and we asked Jesus to show her what happened that caused her to push her husband away. Instantly, Laurie saw herself in the fifth grade. Every day after school, she would go home, do her homework, and have supper. After supper, a girlfriend who lived next door would come over and they would play jacks together.

"What happened, Laurie?"

Laurie said, "My friend never did her homework. Every day, she would copy off my homework before we played jacks. Then, at the end of the year, she won first place for having the best homework."

"What did you conclude, Laurie?"

"Never trust anyone who tries to get close to you. All they want to do is steal your things."

Laurie then recalled a time later in her life when she was in high school and her best friend stole her boyfriend. At that point, we renounced the lies of the enemy and asked Jesus to heal Laurie and wipe out the bad memories. Soon, she had a difficult time remembering the incident. Laurie was rehabilitated. Sadly, however, it was too late to save her marriage.

Waging Spiritual Warfare

A Case Study

In Eastern Malaysia, I met a young girl around twelve years of age during a recess period at the Bible College where I lectured. She was on the verge of death. She was Chinese, but her hair was light brown and she could not eat without throwing up. She reminded me of pictures I had seen of Holocaust victims. She was on the floor with her head on her mother's lap and could hardly stand up and walk.

Through an interpreter I learned that her maternal grandmother raised her from the time she was two years old. Her mother and father were poor and already had three other children they could barely afford to raise. By the time she was ten, her father had a good job and they could afford her, so they came to get the young girl. She was very happy to be back with her parents but she could not hold her food down. No matter what they tried, the most she could do was to suck on bread soaked in milk. She couldn't even swallow the bread.

As I asked her questions, she remembered a time when she was eating in her grandmother's kitchen—she was four or five.

Her grandmother scolded her, "You eat too much, you fat pig! That's why your parents dumped you on me!"

I asked her, "What went through your mind at that time?"

"If my parents take me back, I'm not going to eat so that they won't dump me again."

That lie of the enemy stuck in her mind even though she had only a faint conscious recall of the incident. When her parents finally took her back, her fear of abandonment unconsciously caused her to stop eating. In spite of their constant efforts to feed her and their assurances that they would never be apart again, she simply could not eat.

With the lie of the enemy exposed, I had her renounce the negative suggestion and immediately she was able to eat. I told her that Jesus would never leave her or forsake her, that He would always take care of her needs so that she never needed to be afraid of rejection or abandonment. I told her that nothing could ever separate her from the love of God. She was able to hug and kiss her parents, who reinforced that positive statement by telling her that she could eat all she wanted and they would never leave her. The little family wept and hugged each other.

During the next recess, I checked on her and found her in the cafeteria eating her first full meal in two years. Within a year, she gained weight and was a tireless worker. Her hair had turned black again, and she could eat anything put before her.

Two years later, I returned to Malaysia. I was sitting in a car when a tall, young girl with dark black hair waved vigorously at me.

"Do you know who she is?" my host asked. "She's the girl that almost died of anorexia nervosa a few years ago."

God had set her free from the lies of the evil one. This is an example of suppressed memories actually causing eating disorders such as anorexia nervosa or bulimia.

A CASE STUDY

Shirley had not seen her mother for almost thirty years. When the two finally met again, Shirley was in her mid-forties and had become a Christian. She found her mother to be a delightful person and they established a great relationship—over the telephone. Every time she went to see her mother, however, Shirley could hardly wait to leave. She would bring dinner over but after ten minutes or so she had this penetrating desire to run away. Shirley could not understand it. She enjoyed her mother and wanted to love her but found it impossible.

We asked the Holy Spirit to help Shirley recall the incident that led to all of the feelings that she had. This took her all the way back to when she was around two years old. Shirley loved her father deeply. Her parents were arguing, and Shirley's mother was carrying her. Her mother told her father to get out and never come back. Shirley wanted her father and she reached out and cried for him but her mother held her tight and walked away with her. Her parents obtained a divorce, and Shirley did not see her father for a few years.

Shirley's father eventually took her back at ten years of age, and her mother somewhat abandoned her. Her father raised her from that time on.

"Shirley," I asked, "what emotions and thoughts did you have at that time?"

Shirley answered with her eyes still closed, "I hate my mother for taking me away from my father. I want my daddy!"

"Let's reverse that memory." I had Shirley go back and, instead of hating her mother, I had her hug her mother and say, "I love you, Mother. I forgive you. I renounce the lie of Satan that made me hate my mother. It is not true. I love her and she loves me." Shirley was gently weeping. I walked to the other side of the room to help someone else.

Reversing Negative Agreements

As I kept an eye on Shirley, she began to cough and vomit. Demons of bitterness and hatred were leaving without anyone commanding them to come out. Multitudes of demons of fear, resentment, grief, and anger left. Renouncing the lies took their legal rights away. Shirley coughed and heaved for five minutes.

Later, Shirley gave her testimony: "After things came out of me, I just sat there and waves of joy just swept over me. It was as if something heavy had been lifted off of me. I have never felt so much love for my mother." Genuine love had replaced Shirley's attempt at manufactured love.

MULTIPLE PERSONALITIES

The Bible does not give specific details on techniques for dealing with deep emotional and psychological woundedness. It is difficult to substantiate some of the theories advanced by some Christian counselors on inner healing, but many pastors and counselors who practice inner healing claim that a good number of the people they help seem to have more than one personality.

> The purpose for creating another personality is so the main personality can continue to function in the conscious realm with a minimal amount of pain.

Traumatic incidents can result in the wounded person creating an "inner child," or even "inner children," to wall off hurts. The inner child tends to remain the same age as that of the person when he or she experienced the trauma. Quite often, this other personality has its own emotions, intellect, and personality, separate from those of the person. That way, the child never grows up but continues to absorb the hurts that occurred at an early age. The main personality continues on in life, often oblivious of the inner child, but every so often something triggers memories of the pain, the inner child emerges in the mind, and this adult person begins to act out all the emotions, thoughts, and perceptions of the child. Without warning, grown men and women can suddenly become silly, emotional, rebellious, and irrational for no apparent reason when this inner child comes to the surface.

The purpose for creating another personality is so the main personality can continue to function in the conscious realm with a minimal amount of pain, if any. After all, it was this other inner boy or girl who went through the painful rejection, not the outer person. All the fear, shame, embarrassment, and rejection happened to this "other person," not the main person.

Current circumstances and events can trigger a reaction from the inner children or personalities. In cases where the inner child is well developed, the main personality may suffer memory lapses and forgetfulness of current and past events because the child has taken over the consciousness almost completely. In extreme cases, the two personalities can switch back and forth numerous times within a short period of time.

In their book, *Pigs in the Parlor*, Frank and Ida Mae Hammond claim that in cases of schizophrenia the mind creates a little boy or girl who will absorb all the rejection. They named the personalities Sarah One and Sarah Two. In the Hammonds' experience, Sarah Two, the inner child, has two sides to her personality: a rejection side and a rebellion side.[4]

MERGING PERSONALITIES

Although I have not personally had a lot of experience with multiple personalities, I have had several cases that involved what I refer to as merging personalities. Most of the time, these cases came to me without warning or preparation.

A CASE STUDY

In the Malaysian state of Sarawak, I was walking out the door of a night class when the interpreter asked if I would pray with a young woman. I agreed and walked back into the classroom. There sat a twenty-year-old student, I'll call her Narissa, looking shy and withdrawn. Narissa told me that her mother had hated her father and planned to divorce him when the younger of her two sons reached the age of ten. However, when the boy turned nine, the mother found herself pregnant with a girl—Narissa, the student who sat before me. From the time she was born, Narissa was utterly rejected and treated cruelly by her mother.

She remembered a time when she was five years old and her mother grabbed her arm and pointed out a mangy dog.

"See that dog?" her mother said. "That's your mother! I'm not your mother!"

Narissa wept bitterly.

As we talked, God showed Narissa that she had agreed with (believed) the lies of the devil. She believed that nobody loved her. She believed that she was ugly. Together, we renounced the lies of the devil and recited Scriptures on the love of God.

For I am persuaded that neither death nor life, nor angels nor principalities nor powers, nor things present nor things to come, nor height nor depth, nor any other created thing, shall be able to separate us from the love of God which is in Christ Jesus our Lord. (Romans 8:38–39)

I will not leave you nor forsake you. (Joshua 1:5)

Lo, I am with you always, even to the end of the age.
(Matthew 28:20)

He chose us in Him before the foundation of the world, that we should be holy and without blame before Him in love, having predestined us to adoption as sons by Jesus Christ to Himself, according to the good pleasure of His will.
(Ephesians 1:4–5)

When Narissa knew these things in her heart, I asked her to go back in her mind to the scene with the dog and look for Jesus. She closed her eyes. I told her that sometimes He comes as a bright light or as a person, and other times as a presence. Sure enough, she saw Jesus standing there with His arms open.

"Run to Him," I said, "and let Jesus hug you and tell you how much He loves you."

I had the interpreter hug the young lady. Both wept tears of joy.

Next I tried to directly address the other personality: "Little Narissa, thank you for helping Big Narissa. She doesn't need you anymore to protect her from her mother's rejection. Do you want Little Narissa to merge with Big Narissa?" The girl nodded. I prayed, "Dear Jesus, will You please merge Little Narissa with Big Narissa?"

From a sitting position, the girl flew back as if something had picked her up and tossed her over three rows of chairs, where she fell into a heap. She stood up and her face was like the face of an angel. A big and beautiful smile lit up her face and suddenly this very plain, tormented girl turned into a beautifully radiant and joyful young woman. There was a physical change in her countenance. The next day, Narissa was in class as a very different person. Her physical expression and personality had changed. She was whole again.

The Bible does not go into detail about schizophrenia or mental or emotional illness, although James 1:8 refers to *"a double-minded man, unstable in all his ways."* This type of imagery is understandable since psychiatry and psychology were not known sciences at the time. The Greek word for *double-minded* actually means "two-spirited; vacillating in opinion or purpose." On further inspection, however, the word *spirited* derives from the Greek word *psuche*, which means "mind, soul." Is it referring to two souls or a fragmented soul? We do not really know, and perhaps it is not important.

WITCHCRAFT

Witchcraft involves the manipulation and control of the minds of people against their will. Can witchcraft steal away or control fragments of one's mind? God seems to say, "Yes!":

Thus says the Lord GOD: "Woe to the women who sew magic charms on their sleeves and make veils for the heads of people of every height to hunt souls! Will you hunt the souls of My people, and keep yourselves alive? And will you profane Me among My people for handfuls of barley and for pieces of bread, killing people who should *not die, and keeping people alive who should not live, by your lying to My people who listen to lies?" Therefore thus says the Lord GOD: "Behold, I am against your magic charms by which you hunt souls there like birds. I will tear them from your arms, and let the souls go, the souls you hunt like birds. I will also tear off your veils and deliver My people out of your hand, and they shall no longer be as prey in your hand. Then you shall know that I am the LORD. Because with **lies** you have made the **heart** of the righteous sad, whom I have not made sad; and you have strengthened the hands of the wicked, so that he does not turn from his wicked way to save his life. Therefore you shall no longer envision futility nor practice divination; for I will deliver My people out of your hand, and you shall know that I am the LORD."*

(Ezekiel 13:18–23, emphasis added)

I have had cases where the subject's parents were Satanists. When I prayed that God would send angels to pick up and restore the fragments of that person's soul that were stolen away through witchcraft, the person suddenly sat up and exclaimed that his or her mind became clear in that very instant. I can only believe that the fragments of their mind had been restored.

A person can have parts of his or her personality separated or split because of trauma. A woman who has suffered ritual or sexual abuse at an early age may suffer from loss of memory because of the hurt. The mind copes with these extreme forms of rejection and hurt by blocking off the portion of the mind that contains the hurtful memories—a partial amnesia. Prayer can jog the mind and retrieve the memory. When that happens, you will find a terrified child with all the emotional scars and even physical pains behind that memory. That child is a fragmented piece of the whole soul, separated by the mechanics of the mind in order to cope with the hurt. The mind is in denial, saying, "I haven't been hurt; someone else was hurt—that little child, not me."

Once, as I prayed for a pastor suffering from rejection, I had a vision of a small boy surrounded by icy walls that were eight feet high and three feet thick. The boy would stick his head outside one of the openings in the wall, but as soon as people appeared, the little boy would pull back into the self-imposed prison. Within these walls is the part of the soul or mind we call the "inner child." This may explain why some people have "cold" personalities. They do not trust people and automatically put up walls and withdraw. They find it hard to trust people and rarely have good friends. When the rejection spirit left the pastor, I immediately had a vision of a man in a park holding a large bunch of balloons. The balloons were suddenly released and floated into the sky above the clouds.

> Unforgiveness and bitterness play a large role in poisoning the mind and attitudes of the rejected person.

ROOT OF BITTERNESS

In handling cases of multiple and split personalities (some call them "alters" or "alter personalities"), unforgiveness and bitterness play a large role in poisoning the mind and attitudes of the rejected person. Women, in general, tend to become bitter when rejected. Men, on the other hand, tend to become fearful. If the root of rejection is allowed to grow, many other spirits can enter.

Hebrews 12:14–15 says,

Pursue peace with all people, and holiness, without which no one will see the Lord: looking carefully lest anyone fall short of the grace of God; lest any root of bitterness springing up cause trouble, and by this many become defiled.

Indeed, bitterness opens doors to resentment, anger, hostility, hatred, unforgiveness, retaliation, and even murder and suicide. Imagine the state of mind of a person with all of these spirits.

Some Techniques for Recalling Memories

You may find the following techniques useful after praying and asking the Holy Spirit to bring back the offending memory:

1. If possible, put the counselee in strange or unfamiliar surroundings. A comfortable and secure environment can cause the human mind to clamp down and refuse to recall insecure thoughts or memories. When a person is in an insecure place or circumstances, the mind will open up and often trigger the traumatic memories of rejection, hurt, and pain.

2. Pray and ask the Holy Spirit to reveal the memory. Then ask the counselee to look at his or her body with his or her mind's eye and see if there is any strange sensation he or

she can detect—a tingling, numbness, pain, odor, etc. If they see anything, ask them to concentrate on the problem and on the area of sensation. Often, the memory will resurface at this point. In some cases, the hurts of the past are already manifesting, and the memory of the hurtful event surfaces almost instantly.

> The human mind sometimes reacts to two opposite and irreconcilable problems by shutting itself off from reality.

3. At other times, it is helpful to instruct the person to answer your questions immediately without thinking rationally about the answer. Instruct him or her to say out loud the first thought that comes to mind. Ask, "How old are you? Where are you? Who's there with you? What else is there in the room? What's happening? Who said what? How do you feel?" Insist that he or she answers quickly, even though the response the mind gives may seem ridiculous.

4. The ultimate questions are: What agreement or decision did you make because of what happened? What agreement with yourself did you make? What did you conclude because of this experience?

Have the person enunciate the agreement or belief that was formed because of the incident:

"I'm horrible; I don't deserve to be loved."

"Never trust an older person again."

"Don't let people get close to you. They will always steal your things."

"You can't trust men (or women). Don't let them get close to you."

"I hate my mother (or father, etc.) because she hates me and has rejected my love."

"Don't get close to dogs. They will bite you."

"No one loves me, they will abandon me. They left me alone."

"I'm no good. I caused my parents' divorce."

"My parents don't love me because they got divorced and didn't love me enough to stay together."

"My father doesn't love me because he doesn't spend time with me or talk to me."

"My parents don't love me because they don't pay attention to me or attend my ball games or concerts."

These are just a few examples of negative agreements that I have come across. When the negative agreements have been exposed, have the person renounce and reverse them immediately. Then, have the person go back to the same incident and reshape it into something positive.

Find the positive truth in the Bible. Pray that the Holy Spirit will reveal truth that will destroy the lies of the enemy. The Holy Spirit, the Spirit of truth, will lead us into all truth. (See John 16:13.) Truth destroys the lies of the enemy and frees people.

A CASE STUDY OF CATATONIA

A few years ago, I received a request to pray for a young woman in a remote area of the northern Philippines. When we arrived at her home, I found an attractive nineteen-year-old girl just sitting and staring into space. If you waved your hand six inches in front of her face she would not blink an eye. If you called her name, she would struggle to say something but was unable to respond. She had been like that for a few months. Her parents had called in Catholic priests and even a witch doctor, thinking that someone had put a curse on her. No one was able to help her. When I saw her, the Holy Spirit put the word *catatonia* in my mind.

I knew that the human mind sometimes reacts to two opposite and irreconcilable problems by shutting itself off from reality. Solving one of the problems only creates another, and the mind reacts by locking up.

Her parents told me that she had been living in Manila with her older brother, who had paid for her high school education. When she graduated, he found a job for her, and she agreed to start paying him back. The job was in a produce company, and she worked in the refrigerated section. Every day, she had to pile on thick clothing to ward off the cold. It was miserable. In addition, the older employees picked on her incessantly. She hated the job, and after two months, she quit.

When she quit, her brother became furious, accusing her of being ungrateful. After a week, she went back to the job but after another two weeks she could stand it no longer. To avoid her brother, she packed up her belongings and caught a bus home while he was away at work. At home, she had insomnia for two weeks and then fell into her current state of catatonia.

I had her parents call her brother in Manila and explain the situation. We put the phone next to her ear and the brother spoke to her. He forgave her and told her that it was okay for her to quit her job. He also told her that she could find a better job. Her parents and other family members also told her that it was okay for her to quit and that they would help her. The next morning, she came out of her trance. Her problems may not have been solved, but the possible solutions were no longer in opposition to each other.

UNDERSTANDING THE HUMAN MIND

Often, when a person faces deep problems that he or she cannot solve, the mind resorts to fear, depression, amnesia, forgetfulness, denial, catatonia, and other conditions. When you experience cases like these, you know that the person is most likely facing problems in life where the solutions seem impossible to find or carry out. In response, the mind shuts down. Helping people to see and untangle the solutions to their problems can be the key to their deliverance. In cases like these, the problems can manifest in uncharacteristic or illogical behavior.

Sometimes, a person has a physical ailment that is chronic (asthma, rash, allergies, etc.), or perhaps he or she has engaged in undesirable behavior (adultery, promiscuity, an addiction to pornography, uncontrolled rage, etc.). Upon questioning people such as this, I often discover that their father or mother had the same ailment or exhibited similar behavior. Often there was some kind of prominent problem in the family. For instance, the mother and father did not get along because of the father's adulterous affair. The mother let all the children know about their father's terrible offense and made it clear that the children should ostracize him. Very often, later in their adult lives, those children end up engaging in the same adulterous behavior. Despite their father's actions, the children loved him, but their mother refused to allow them to show it. Therefore, in an effort to justify loving their father, the child or children commit the same offense. Now they could love father because they were on the same level. Once such a lie is uncovered and renounced, the desire for extramarital affairs disappears or is diminished. Often, spirits of adultery and fornication leave at that point.

A Case Study

Sometimes, incomplete relationships continue to follow a person and begin to manifest in negative ways. In Fiji, a pastor in his fifties came to me in secret one day. He admitted that he needed help with a terrible temper. His wife frequently told him that if people ever found out about his temper tantrums at home, he would lose his position as pastor. As he was speaking to me, I heard the Holy Spirit say, "Unfair!" As soon as I conveyed this to the man, he started sobbing. He told me that when he was six years old his father died. By the time he was ten, his mother had remarried and had three children with her new husband. Since he was older than his half sisters and brother, his stepfather picked on him incessantly. He had to do all the hard work on the farm while the others did very little. His stepfather harassed him all the time and never thanked him or gave him gifts. He was so upset that he left home at eighteen and never returned. Since that time, his stepfather had died.

I invited him to talk to Jesus and to say the things that he was never able to say to his stepfather. Just to be clear, I stated that he was talking to Jesus—not his dead stepfather. I asked him to express his hurt, disappointment, and anger. I walked out of the office and closed the door. Half an hour later, the pastor opened the door. His eyes were red from crying, but he told me that he had gotten everything off his shoulders and ended up forgiving his stepfather and telling him that he loved him.

A year later, the pastor was at the airport to pick me up. As we drove away, he said, "I asked to pick you up because I wanted to thank you. Since that day in the office, I haven't had a single temper attack or depression."

A CASE STUDY

Another pastor had recurring backaches for over fifteen years. He had been to see doctors, acupuncturists, and masseurs almost on a weekly basis. Though he occasionally experienced temporary relief, the back pain never completely left him. Prayer and even deliverance were not able to heal him.

The Holy Spirit directed me to have the pastor tell Jesus all the things he wanted to say to his father. For more than thirty minutes, the young man laid it all out before Jesus— the hurts, the unsaid things, the sadness and grief, the happy times, everything. When he was through, it was as though a weight had been lifted off his shoulders. As if that wasn't enough, his back pain was completely gone.

The pastor wondered why his sore back disappeared, so we prayed and asked God to reveal what happened in his past that brought about a sore back. He suddenly recalled the trauma of his father's death when he was fifteen years old. He had received a telephone call that his father had suffered a heart attack and was in the intensive care unit. Before he could get to the hospital, his father died. He never had the chance to say good-bye. The pastor played football, and his father had attended every game. After each game, the father would scold him and point out all of his mistakes. After a while, the young boy resented his father. At the funeral, the pastor was unable to shed a tear over his father's passing.

Reversing Negative Agreements

The pastor recalled that his father had a sore back, too. He remembered massaging his father's back many times. Those were the only occasions that this pastor felt needed and loved by his father. The sudden loss of his father left him with an unresolved hole in his life. He needed to tell his father how much he loved and missed him. The sore back was merely what his mind latched onto. It represented a bridge between the two men, but now it was no longer needed as their relationship was now complete. The pastor had told his father everything that needed to be said. Not only did the sore back disappear, but also his recurring headaches and depression did, too.

MY OWN CASE

My own father died in my arms of a heart attack when I was eighteen years old. Like the pastor, I never had the opportunity to tell him how much I loved him. He left like an evening breeze.

He remained in my thoughts, though, and for fifteen years or so I would dream about him at least once a week. Finally, I sat down and told Jesus everything I had ever wanted to say to my father—the good and the bad, my disappointment in his dying, and the fact that my dreams of a medical career had come to a screeching halt when he died. Through Jesus, I told my father that I loved him and that I forgave him. Immediately, I received the feeling that he forgave and loved me in return. From that time forward, I never dreamed of my father again—not once.

Telling Jesus the things you've never been able to tell someone who hurt you is not some kind of mental trick. I firmly believe that Jesus can actually take the things you say and complete the relationship you had with that other person and bring a sense of closure to such unresolved conflict. In the words of the psalmist: *"The LORD redeems the soul of His servants"* (Psalm 34:22). He will take whatever is broken and make it new again.

A CASE STUDY

Margaret lived in Hawaii and had not talked to her sister for fifteen years, even though she lived in Los Angeles and visited the islands every few years. Margaret admitted that she could not even remember what their disagreement was about.

I had Margaret invite Jesus to take the place of her younger sister and then to say what was on her heart.

> In many cases, expressing hurt and pain to the other person after so many years may not solve the problem and may even exacerbate it.

"Oh, honey," she began, "I'm so sorry we fought. I don't even remember what we fought about. Please forgive me. I forgive you. I love you."

It was that simple. Afterward, there was no immediate sign of relief or change, so we prayed and left it at that.

Margaret went home that night, and the phone rang an hour later. It was her younger sister calling from Los Angeles. Her sister initiated the conversation: "Oh, honey, I'm so sorry we fought. I don't even remember what we fought about. Please forgive me. I forgive you. I love you."

Reversing Negative Agreements

ANOTHER CASE STUDY

The nineteen-year-old daughter of a new member of our church came to see me one afternoon. She had been the apple of her father's eye, but then her parents went through a painful divorce. Since that time, she had gotten married and was now seven months pregnant. Yet, she had not talked to her father for five years. An aunt had informed her that her father knew of her pregnancy. Still he didn't call.

After praying and asking Jesus to sit opposite her and take the place of her father, she told Him everything she wanted to tell her father.

"How come you don't even call me? You know I'm pregnant, and you don't even ask how I am, or how the baby is doing."

The very next morning at eight o'clock, the phone rang. It was her father. He said, "Hi, honey. I'm sorry I haven't called you or talked to you. How are you? And how is the baby?"

Where there is an incomplete or broken relationship with many things left unsaid, the mind will sometimes turn these things over and over. It seems that the mind will not be satisfied until everything that needs to be said is said. Allowing Jesus to handle such a situation avoids upsetting the other person (if living) who may not understand, or who may possibly pull further away. In many cases, expressing such hurt and pain to the other person after so many years may not solve the problem and may even exacerbate it. Lay it at the feet of Jesus; let Him take it. Even if the other person is out of reach or deceased, Jesus still *"redeems the soul"* and brings healing.

DO THEY REALLY WANT HEALING?

Sometimes, a person claims to desire healing, but deep down he or she really does not.

A man came to see me one day and sat there shifting around and fidgeting in his chair.

"What's the matter?" I inquired.

"I've got a bad back, and I just came from my doctor's office," he replied.

He claimed that prayer could not heal him and medical treatment did very little. He was a heavy equipment operator and had injured his back eighteen months earlier. He was receiving worker's compensation insurance payments each month that were even higher than his monthly salary when he was working.

"Sounds like a pretty good deal," I said. "Maybe you should keep your sore back. Are you sure you want healing?"

"Of course," he said.

"Look at all the benefits you get for being sick," I explained. "When was the last time you took your wife shopping?"

"I can't. My back is sore," he answered.

"When was the last time you helped clean the house, cut the grass, wash the car, or visited your in-laws?"

"I can't do any of those things," he said. "My back won't allow me."

"Are you sure you want to get healed?" I asked again. "After all, you would have to take your wife shopping, clean the house, cut the grass, wash the car, and visit your in-laws."

Frustrated at my prodding, he finally said aloud, "Yes, I'm willing to do all these things if I could be healed of my sore back."

I then said, "How's your back?"

He grabbed his lower back with both hands and shouted, "Oh my, the pain is gone! I don't feel any pain!"

His mouth claimed to want healing, but his subconscious mind did not. His mind needed to be healed before his back.

In John 5, we find Jesus at the pool called Bethesda. At the pool were many sick people because it was known that an angel would occasionally come down and stir up the waters. It was said that instant healing would come to whoever entered the pool first. An invalid sat by the pool who had suffered in his infirmity for thirty-eight years.

Knowing of the man's condition, Jesus asked the man, *"Do you want to be made well?"* (verse 6). In other words, "Do you really want to be healed?" Why did Jesus even have to ask? The man could well have answered, "Sir, I don't come here to socialize. Why else would I be here for?"

That question penetrated the man's subconscious mind and wiped out any hesitation or resistance of his mind towards his healing. It caused him to affirm his intention and desire. As a result, the man received his healing. (See John 5:8–9.)

CHAPTER FOUR

HINDRANCES TO THE ANOINTING

If you possess the anointing to participate in spiritual deliverance, that anointing will always exist. There are, however, certain factors that can diminish the anointing and affect the outcome. One such element that I will address further in a later chapter is unbelief. When there are people in the room who do not believe in demonic activity, deliverance can be stifled. Scripture warns us, *"Do not quench the Spirit"* (1 Thessalonians 5:19). The absence of anointing for deliverance has occurred only four times in my career. Each time, a group of people in the audience did not believe that there are such things as demons, or they didn't believe that Christians could have demons.[5]

Another factor is stubbornness or pride. I have seen Christians utterly refuse to participate in a deliverance service in any way. They refuse to pray or even close their eyes. Perhaps they refuse to consider that evil spirits might be affecting them, or perhaps they do not want to make a scene before others. Invariably, they do not enter in and do not receive any deliverance, even while people around them are experiencing great freedom and release. A person who does not want deliverance usually does not receive it.

Usually, pastors and their wives are the first to jump up in front of their congregation and say, "Me first! I want deliverance!" Others, on the other hand, will pretend that they have something else to do and they walk out of the room. Some pastors and church leaders make believe that they are untouched by demons and intend to merely assist in the deliverance session. This can also quench the Spirit of deliverance.

> A person who does not want deliverance usually does not receive it.

Once, when I was teaching, two old women in the back of the room were chatting and laughing. They were not paying attention. I felt the presence of God in that room just fading away. When the anointing is there, my words are smooth and connected; when the anointing is missing, I start stammering and forgetting what to say. I immediately stopped teaching and informed the group that the Holy Spirit was grieved, and we needed to repent. As we prayed and repented, the presence returned. The body of Christ needs to reverence the Holy Spirit.

There are several spirits that the devil can send to settle on a congregation, on church boards, or on individual church leaders. These spirits can overlap in their effectiveness and can often be found together. Each one is strong and effective enough to stifle the work of the Holy Spirit in the lives of believers. In the end, you can't wait them out, hoping they will leave. They must be driven out through spiritual deliverance and prayer.

THE SPIRIT OF LEGALISM

Resistance to deliverance can be unintentional but nonetheless sufficient to kill or hamper the anointing. One such form of resistance is legalism, or formalism. Legalism implies a rigidity or strict adherence to the laws and rules of man—a type of "Pharisee spirit." It says:

"You cannot do this. You cannot do that."

"You must do this. You must do that."

I'm all for maintaining a proper order in things, but in an environment of strict legalism, I have found that there is very little room for the Holy Spirit to move. There is more of a reliance on the things of men rather than the things of the Spirit.

The spirit of legalism can destroy the anointing, especially during public deliverance services. Legalism finds its strength in the spirit of pride, which often masks unbelief. When people hear that Christians cannot have demons, they may not believe in the casting out of devils and resist it in their heart. Sometimes, during a deliverance service, believers will sit in their chairs, mentally objecting to everything I say because of unbelief. I have had interpreters stubbornly refuse to translate my words because they did not agree with my theology.

Pride causes one to promote his or her ideas as the "only true way." Pride says, "My way is the right way and the only way. Therefore, if you want to grow in God, you must listen to me. I know how to get there, and I will show you how. But make sure you stick to the rules I give you."

Pride is an attitude that refuses to consider other points of view or beliefs. I have been to churches that do not believe that Christians can have demons, and there was absolutely no anointing. Even when some of the people in the church were open-minded, the ruling spirit over the church prevented deliverance from taking place. The leaders were suspicious and argumentative and the saints were cautious and afraid to ask questions. They hesitated to come up for prayer after the service.

> Legalism finds its strength in the spirit of pride, which often masks unbelief.

When you walk into a church with that kind of attitude, you can sense it in the spirit. I once went to teach at a church in Singapore. No one smiled, greeted me, or shook my hand. I told some well-tested jokes and nobody laughed or even smiled. Our team sang a few songs and there was no clapping or smiling. The audience was quiet and nonresponsive. There was a sense of fear in the place; it was spiritually dead. There was no liberty in the Holy Spirit. Teaching was like walking knee-deep in a swamp. There was absolutely no anointing for deliverance. A day later I learned from another pastor that the leaders of that church taught that Christians could not have demons.

Two days later, I walked into another church and immediately sensed the presence of the Holy Spirit. The people there were praying earnestly and weeping before the Lord. The saints greeted us warmly and informally, they responded freely to my jokes, and there was a warm, loving atmosphere. When we praised God in song, they clapped with genuine enthusiasm. The leaders were open and anxious to learn more. The saints came up to us afterward and asked many questions. The deliverance we experienced there was incredible.

THE SPIRIT OF FORMALISM

Years ago, I was invited to teach at a Bible college in Vanuatu. As I entered the campus, there were many students standing around. But as we walked into the building, no one came forth to shake hands or greet my group. As the leader escorted me into the classroom, I noticed that no one was smiling and many appeared afraid to even look me in the eye.

This was a Pentecostal college, and yet during praise and worship almost no one raised their hands. Instead the students and faculty seemed stiff and formal. The songs were old-time hymns, but there was no clapping or animation. During my first break in teaching, no one came forward to ask questions, which is highly unusual.

When I asked the pastor what was going on in the religious community of the city, he immediately told me that a group of evangelicals very much controlled the town. Their services were highly organized. But it all seemed to stem from one particular event.

Since their country was a Christian country, different denominations took turns handling certain government dedications and events. The government asked him to conduct the blessing of the new airport and, typical of Pentecostal churches, his church did not "dress up" for the occasion. There were loud "Alleluias!" and "Amens." There was shouting, clapping, jumping, dancing, and hand raising to accompany the singing. Instead of gowns, ribbons, and uniforms that other clergy wore, this pastor wore an ordinary suit. As a result, he was widely criticized for his disrespectful dress, as well as the unruly behavior of his congregation during praise and worship. They criticized him for having no order or ceremonies worth attending.

Before long, the Pentecostal churches began dressing up their leaders in colorful gowns. Their services changed. They began parading up the aisle to the altar with acolytes and a choir trailing as the congregation dressed to kill. There's nothing wrong with these things individually. What was twisted was the way that all the churches in the town tried to outdo each other in pageantry and color. It was truly form over function. How things appeared on the outside took precedence over what God wanted to do on the inside. Slowly, the born-again Christians began to take on the deadness that comes from spiritual pride. You could hear the words of Jesus: *"Woe to you, scribes and Pharisees, hypocrites! For you are like whitewashed tombs which indeed appear beautiful outwardly, but inside are full of dead men's bones and all uncleanness"* (Matthew 23:27).

As I spoke with the pastor that day at the Bible college, he immediately understood what I was talking about and agreed to try to break the spirits of formalism and legalism over their Bible college and church. When we returned from the break, I explained to the students what I discerned, and we began to sing and dance with wild abandon. In the beginning, the students seemed afraid to react and participate, but as their pastor began to dance and sing, they slowly entered in. Within a few songs, we were all jumping up and down, clapping hands, and dancing. The change was dramatic! The Holy Spirit was indeed present. There were smiles and laughter, deep joy and fellowship—and so much more liberty. The spirit of formalism had been bound and defeated.

Far too many Pentecostal churches in America have fallen into the same trap of reverting back to formalism and legalism. Afraid of standing out as different, they choose instead to conform to the deadness of other churches. Several churches I recently visited in California exhibited the same formalism that I had experienced in Vanuatu. The congregation seemed afraid to raise their hands to heaven and sing or speak in tongues. Everything had to be reserved and proper.

Once, a San Diego pastor invited me to teach about spiritual warfare at his church. My seminars usually last two to four full days. In this case, however, when I arrived the pastor informed me that I had only fifteen minutes to preach—any longer and the congregation would complain. I was to arrive at least thirty minutes before the service to greet the people, and I was to wear a blue and white gown and participate in the opening processional. After my talk (I cheated by going almost twenty-five minutes), the pastor told me to make sure that I quickly accompanied him down the center aisle of the church so we could thank the people for attending.

We were invited to a spaghetti lunch in the church cafeteria where the pastor asked me if I would address a group of fifteen members because they were curious. Meanwhile, he was off to teach a men's Bible class.

I agreed and took the group into a small classroom. I knew that I had to do something major as soon as possible. I began by asking if anyone needed healing. An elderly woman raised her hand. She had suffered from a sore back for more than two years and could not sit or stand for long. I had her limp up to the front where I was sitting. She bent over in pain. I opened my Bible to Matthew 12:15, which says, "[Jesus] *withdrew from there. And great multitudes followed Him, and He healed them all.*"

I looked the woman in the eye and told her: "*All* means *all*; all means everybody, and everybody includes you! Isn't that right?"

"Yes," the elderly woman agreed.

"How's your back?" I asked.

She moved around and bent over. Then she exclaimed, "O my, the pain is gone! Alleluia!"

A few minutes later, the janitor walked in and announced that he had to close the windows and lock the place up. I informed the group, "Why don't we go and sit in the courtyard outside, and we can continue with our teaching on spiritual warfare and healing?" I gathered my things and took a moment to call my wife. When I went out into the courtyard a few minutes later, no one was there, and the parking lot was empty!

They had seen a major miracle and were learning about a subject not many had heard before, but their routines did not allow them to stay any longer. They were off to do other things.

THE SPIRIT OF FALSE APPEARANCES

Some years ago, I prayed and asked God why the body of Christ on earth is so weak. Suddenly, I had a vision of the yellow pages of a telephone directory. An index finger appeared and pointed to a word at the upper right-hand corner of the open directory. As the word came into focus, it said: "Appearances."

The message to me was that too many within the body of Christ cover up their lack of power and truth by putting out false appearances, pretenses, and façades, making believe that everything is still holy and spiritually blessed. Many saints pretend to be spiritually mature by quoting Scriptures and saying the right phrases in church. They go through the motions of honoring God and His church, but it is only a façade. They are like a model cake on display in the front window of the local bakery—the frosting looks beautiful, but beneath it is only cardboard. It is a cover-up for the lack of righteousness and maturity.

Before Sunday service a few weeks later, I was standing in the back of the church when a member came up to me and said, "Pastor, I had a dream. Can you interpret it for me?" I agreed and she related the following:

> I was with another woman. There was a small church building in the middle of a jungle, surrounded by a high fence. The other woman and I decided to check out the jungle, so we sneaked out and walked along a path. We heard the roar of a lion, so we hid behind a tree. When we peeked at the lion, a dead lamb was in his mouth and he was tossing it into the air and catching it. He was just playing with it. We got scared, so we ran back to the church. As we were running, the other woman tripped on a rock and her face fell into a thick bush. When she stood up, white powder completely covered her face.

Before I could give an interpretation, the music began, signaling the start of the service. I informed the woman that I would talk with her after the service. As I stood at the back of the room, I discerned that there was absolutely no anointing in the room. It was spiritually dead. After the third song, I was so frustrated in my spirit that I walked to the front, grabbed a microphone, and started praying and binding up spirits. Then I returned to the back of the room and the music started up again. This time, however, the presence of the Holy Spirit was very strong.

After the service, another member came up to me and said,

Pastor, when the music started, I saw a vision of a fat lady sitting in front. She had on a black-and-white polka-dot dress, but the white dots kept getting small and then big and then small again. She wore a bright red wig and long earrings. She also had a large pair of dark eyeglasses with frames covered in fancy jewels. She had long false eyelashes, thick white powder on her face, and large red circles on her cheeks, almost like a circus clown. I looked down at her feet and she had tiny feet encased in beautiful shoes.

Then I saw you walk up to the front and as you were praying, I saw a huge angel stand behind you. When I looked for the woman, she was gone. What does that mean?

God was still answering my prayers. The woman in the polka-dot dress was a demon of false pretenses and deception. The real person hides behind a red wig, false eyelashes, ornate eyeglasses, long earrings, thick makeup, and small shoes.

The spirit of false appearances was fat because it was prospering in the church. Many had fallen for her charms.

Hindrances to the Anointing

The black-and-white polka-dot dress with the white dots alternately expanding and shrinking represents typical saints today. When they go to church, they act holy and the white dot expands. When they go home they are not so holy, and the white dot shrinks. It is all pretense and phoniness—shadow with no substance.

Even the tiny feet in the vision had meaning. Tradition has it that a Chinese emperor had a dream of a beautiful goddess dancing with tiny feet. He was so enamored by the small feet that his people adopted them as a standard for beauty. They began to bind up the feet of their infant daughters until they were past the age of puberty. When they placed shoes on the feet of these girls, it was beautiful. But the feet were deformed and ugly—broken and twisted with toes bent under the soles. They could hardly walk and were permanently disabled. Take the shoes off, and the truth was grotesque.

Someone once said, "You can fool some of the people all of the time, and you can fool all of the people some of the time; but you cannot fool all of the people all of the time." When it comes to God, you cannot fool Him for even one second!

The first lady's dream was the same. Christians who pretend to be holy and spiritually mature but in reality are not are only lambs in the kingdom of God. They are easy prey for Satan because they are all show and have no spiritual strength. Satan is able to toss them around and play with them before devouring the helpless lambs. The woman that tripped represents phony Christians who will one day fall and be exposed. White powder covers their true condition, like cosmetics covers blemishes and wrinkles on the face.

The spirits of legalism and formalism include false appearances, façades, pretenses, and make-believe forms of Christianity. Rituals, man-made rules, customs, and traditions can cover up the fact that there is little spiritual understanding or power in the body of Christ today. The church has covered up its lack of power and spiritual maturity with all the accoutrements of prosperity and well-being. Sometimes it seems that there is little truth at all left in the church today.

> The church has covered up its lack of power and spiritual maturity with all the accoutrements of prosperity and well-being.

The church that God originally gave us was devoid of phony pageantry, feel-good ceremonies, and many of the customs we associate with "church" today. They were real and truthful before God. I fear that one day we will pay the price for our current charade.

THE SPIRIT OF RELIGIOUS PRIDE

Religious pride can literally cover a church like a wet blanket. The atmosphere then becomes stifling, and there is virtually no liberty. You can spiritually discern it and sometimes people actually have physical difficulty breathing. Religious pride can snuff out revival. Believers find it difficult to pray and read the Word, and their praise and worship is dry and forced. Sometimes it is "a sluggard spirit." Some deliverance pastors claim that it is also the "spirit of Orion," a form of religious pride.

Once, as we plowed through a service that was dry and dead, God suddenly gave a woman a vision. In the vision, the woman was in a dark room and boards covered all the windows and doors. On one side, she saw a large slug inching its way up the wall, leaving a slimy trail behind it. She peered through the boards on the door and saw bright sunlight. Just outside the door, a white dove walked around.

The interpretation was obvious. The sluggard spirit had locked everyone up, and there was no liberty in the Holy Spirit. The sunlight and white dove represented light, truth, and the Holy Spirit. Spiritual pride keeps God's people locked up in jail.

In such a situation, the Holy Spirit cannot move because He cannot (or more accurately will not) even get inside the room to anoint the saints. The saints have allowed an atmosphere of complacency and self-righteousness to enter the church.

As we were praying one morning during that period, we had a vision of a huge slug—about ten feet long—just lying in the middle of the floor. The prayers that day were dry, and there seemed to be no anointing. When we repented and bound up the spirit of pride and sluggardness, the anointing returned.

Job 41 speaks of Leviathan, the spirit of pride. Air cannot enter his tightly bound scales. *"His rows of scales are his pride, shut up tightly as with a seal; one is so near another that no air can come between them"* (Job 41:15–16). *Spirit* means "pneuma," "air," or "breath." The Holy Spirit will not get past the scales of pride.

THE SPIRIT OF INTELLECTUALISM

Another form of legalism is an attitude that says:

I graduated from Bible college and have a master's degree in theology. Here is what I think, and no one can convince me otherwise. If you don't agree with what I teach, you are in error and in danger of losing your salvation—or at the least you are sinning and displeasing God.

In such an atmosphere, congregations become afraid and unwilling to allow themselves to be exposed to teaching that is in any way contrary to what their leader teachers—no matter how biblical it is. Even if you get the opportunity to preach there, as soon as you leave the pastor dilutes or wipes out everything you said by pointing out the "errors" in your teaching according to his own interpretation. Such a controlling leader cannot afford to let his flock think that he is wrong; therefore, he looks for every little thing to discredit you. This kind of mind control is a type of witchcraft. It is often seen in cults, but unfortunately can also be found within God's church. In most cases, it goes totally unrecognized by the persons in the church, but it is present nevertheless.

Intellectualism is a form of legalism. Where it is present, there is a lack of Holy Spirit anointing; all that's there is only a form of earthly wisdom and intelligence. Every year, "spiritual" men and women write and distribute tons of books. Some are Spirit-filled; however, many are filled the spirit of intellectualism instead the Spirit of God.

Knowledge of the Word of God is not equal to godly, spiritual wisdom. Many students study religion in college and can quote Scriptures with the best Christians, but that does not turn them into experts or even into believers. Many pastors have a form of holiness based on knowledge. Congregations become infatuated with pastors who have letters and degrees after their name, as if somehow they are closer to the throne of God. They are full of Greek and Hebrew word definitions and doctrinal positions, but it covers up the fact that they are as spiritually dry as an old bone. They spout eschatology, homiletics, and sacerdotal affairs, but they do not know God. I know of one religion professor at a university who claims to have read through the entire Bible over one hundred times, yet he remains an atheist. False façades and pretense often prevent people from growing spiritually. True spiritual growth comes through sacrifice, obedience, and humility, not through intellect, pride, and reason.

Intellectual leaders tend to be finicky and dictatorial over the least little things. They closely control the administration of the church, church staff, and the volunteer leaders. Everything must be perfect. Their church services are tightly planned and scripted, prayers are repetitive, and the programs remain the same, year in and year out. In such a church, changes may take place physically, but seldom spiritually.

Often, the congregation starts to emulate this leadership style. College or seminary degrees become of ultimate importance. Those with the proper credentials and background are the only people deemed worthy to speak publicly or lead. Those with a mere bachelor's degree are seen as inferior to someone with a master's degree. In some South Pacific and Asian countries, people will not waste time listening to anyone who does not hold a number of college degrees. This form of prejudice comes out of the toxin of legalism, and, like a cancer, it can kill the work of the Holy Spirit from the inside out.

THE SPIRIT OF UNBELIEF

Unbelief can also work to quench the Spirit of God. Early on the first day of a spiritual warfare seminar, I like to have people come up front for physical healing. This is to build the faith of people for the next day's deliverance sessions. On one particular occasion in the Philippines, eight people came up for healing and God healed every one of them on the spot. The Holy Spirit was truly moving.

At the end of the second day, however, there was absolutely no anointing for deliverance. As I was pondering what had happened that afternoon, a couple of friends who had attended the seminar reported that a group of six people from a local cult had sneaked in the back door. This cult did not believe in the ministry of the Holy Spirit or in the existence of demons. They sat in the back of the room, snickering and mocking. Their unbelief and arrogance poisoned the room and quenched God's Spirit.

> Unbelief is like a wet blanket that completely smothers faith. It will squelch the Holy Spirit from doing anything miraculous.

On another occasion, a number of pastors who did not agree with what I was saying challenged me. The arguments went around and around for over an hour. When it came time for deliverance, the anointing was flat.

Two years later, I returned and the anointing was incredible. Every person in attendance, there were more than one hundred, experienced great deliverance and healing.

The head pastor remarked to my assistant, "Wow, it wasn't like this the last time he was here!"

Hindrances to the Anointing

My assistant answered, "Yeah, but nobody challenged him this time, either."

Unbelief will kill God's anointing. In Luke 8:49–56, we find the following episode:

> *While He was still speaking, someone came from the ruler of the synagogue's house, saying to him, "Your daughter is dead. Do not trouble the Teacher." But when Jesus heard it, He answered him, saying, "Do not be afraid; only believe, and she will be made well." When He came into the house, He permitted no one to go in except Peter, James, and John, and the father and mother of the girl. Now all wept and mourned for her; but He said, "Do not weep; she is not dead, but sleeping." And they ridiculed Him, knowing that she was dead. But He put them all outside, took her by the hand and called, saying, "Little girl, arise." Then her spirit returned, and she arose immediately. And He commanded that she be given something to eat. And her parents were astonished, but He charged them to tell no one what had happened.*

Unbelief is like a wet blanket that completely smothers faith. It will squelch the Holy Spirit from doing anything miraculous. As Jesus did above, the only thing you can do is remove those with unbelief. As Jesus said in another episode, *"A prophet is not without honor except in his own country and in his own house"* (Matthew 13:57). When you stand in faith on the power of God, be prepared for family, friends, and those familiar with you to have a built-in resistance and unbelief.

Deliverance should always work. If the anointing is absent, you can be sure that there is an evil spirit at work somewhere. Talk to other leaders. Talk to others in the room. Discern which spirit or spirits are interfering with the work of God. Is it intellectualism? Is it legalism or formalism? Is it religious pride or plain old unbelief? Identify it and publicly drive it out in Jesus' name!

CHAPTER FIVE

ANGELS

There are many good books about angels, so I will try not to be redundant. Instead, I will attempt to stick to my own personal experiences and understanding of the angelic realm.

PROTECTION OF THE SAINTS

Children have angels protecting them. Jesus said in Matthew 18:10, *"Take heed that you do not despise one of these little ones, for I say to you that in heaven their angels always see the face of My Father who is in heaven."* Therefore, according to Scripture, we know that God assigns guardian angels to watch over His little ones. Over the years, I have personally heard countless tales of children who were rescued from danger and came back telling of an angel who carried or guided them to safety.

It is my experience that God also assigns angels to protect adult believers as well. During a trip to Fiji, we did some heavy spiritual warfare and deliverance. After the evening session, a man walked up to me.

"I used to worship Degei, the god of Fiji," he said, "and I can still hear his voice sometimes. He just told me that he is going to kill you tonight."

On the way back to my cottage, I prayed that God would send angels to protect me that night. When I shut off the lights and went to bed, I saw a huge angel standing over my cottage. He must have been at least twenty-five feet tall and the top of his folded wings reached high above his head. He was so bright that I could not see his facial features, but I could clearly see his outline and the pattern of feathers on the top of his left wing.

That night the electricity was mysteriously cut off. The next morning, one of the students reported seeing many evil spirits trying to attack the Bible college that night. According to the student, they surrounded the campus but could not get into the property because angels also surrounded the college. Unable to enter, the evil spirits were able to cut off the electricity just to show that they had been there.

Hebrews 1:14 says, *"Are they not all ministering spirits sent forth to minister for those who will inherit salvation?"* Angels minister on behalf of the children of God. Angels walk the earth and guard the saints every day. I agree with other experts on healing and deliverance that there are probably a multitude of angels on the earth at any given moment carrying out God's assignments. [6]

ANGELS IN THE PHILIPPINES

We have a mission house and Bible college in the Philippines. The neighborhood there ranges from hostile to unconcerned, although a nearby Roman Catholic Church prays against us and has occasionally marched around our compound with candles and statues. Sometimes someone throws a dead rooster over the fence. On one occasion, we returned home just in time to put out a fire that someone had set in our storage room.

That all stopped, however, the night neighbors reported seeing a tall man dressed in a white robe walk right through our front door. These neighbors were not even believers. Our students and staff occasionally report seeing bright columns of light in the mission house, and our cameras have recorded mysterious, perfect wheels of light in the photos taken of our mission house and crusade meetings. Often, four or five cameras used by different people record the same spinning wheels. These wheels are perfectly symmetrical and of intricate design. This has happened several times over the years. We are convinced that there are many angels guarding us at any given moment.

In early 2006, we were teaching deliverance in a remote province where a wife and her three teenage daughters gave their lives to Christ. The next morning, I heard shouting outside the church. The woman's husband was very angry with us for converting his family and threatened to come back with a bolo knife and cut us up. Nothing happened that day, but two days later the man meekly came up and told us that he was so angry that day he had planned to take his rifle, walk into the church, and shoot holes in the ceiling and floor just to frighten us. However, when he grabbed the rifle, his feet stuck to the floor and he could not move them. He panicked and put the rifle back in its box. When he let go of the rifle he was able to move his two feet again. I believe angels prevented him from taking the lives of others and ruining his own. That day, he accepted Jesus as Lord and Savior.

Whenever you are involved in deliverance and spiritual warfare, God sends His angels to protect and help you.

OTHER ANGELIC APPEARANCES

One day as I was praying and casting out demons, a group of new converts grew frightened at the prospect of evil spirits coming out and attacking them. To alleviate their fears, I prayed aloud and asked God to send His angels to surround and protect us. As I prayed, I propped my right foot on a chair. Then I went back to casting out demons.

When I was through, a woman sitting at the back of the room some distance away walked up to me and asked, "Brother Richard, what were you doing when you had your right foot on the chair?"

"Why?" I asked.

"Because, all of a sudden, I saw a whole bunch of fireflies surrounding the group. They were darting back and forth and looked like they were spinning. Do they have fireflies in Hawaii?" she asked.

"No, they're just angels," I told her.

There have been times when angels have appeared during services. Very often, a tall angel appears behind me and slightly to my left. At other times, more than one angel will appear behind me. This not only happens in my own church but in other churches where I go to lecture on spiritual warfare.

In Hawaii, an angel appeared as I was teaching deliverance at a church I had never been to before. A woman in the congregation who had never known me and probably did not know anything about deliverance saw him. He was so real that she sent her husband backstage during the break to investigate whether there was someone hiding there. She kept exclaiming, "You should see the size of him!"

On other occasions, people witnessed a ring of angels holding arms and circling the room. They were not tall, probably four feet at most, according to those who saw them. They appeared only in outline and as figures of light.

ANGEL HELPERS

In Fiji, I participated in a deliverance service when the pastor himself fell to the floor, shaking. We gathered around him and proceeded to cast out demons as he was lying on the floor. Later, after he had fully recovered, the pastor asked to share his experience with the congregation.

He reported that as he was lying on his back being delivered, a huge angel stepped over him and then stood behind me on the stage. He remembered thinking to himself, *I wonder if it is an angel of light sent by Satan.* At that point, the angel lifted up his visor and smiled. It was like no other smile you have ever seen on earth. The angel was incredibly beautiful.

"I wondered if it was a woman," the pastor said, "but when I looked at his body, his muscles were so huge that it had to be male."

Then the angel pulled his sword out halfway. The sword was so bright that the pastor had to shield his eyes.

The next morning, as the same pastor began his class, he witnessed what seemed to be an entire company of angels entering the room carrying suits of armor. They hung the armor on unseen pegs and stood at the back of the room, talking with one another.

"They were just like you and me," he later told me. "They were looking around, arms folded, and chatting. Then two of them began to measure people the way a tailor would. I think they were taking measurements for the suits of armor they brought with them."

When we go to battle against the kingdom of darkness, we are not alone. God dispatches angels to our side. There are many powerful angels on our side. *If God is for us, who can be against us?"* (Romans 8:31).

> Angels do superhuman feats to protect us; they accompany us on trips, protect us from the evil one, and stand guard around us.

I have witnessed angels manifesting themselves many times during deliverance. Once when I was praying over a woman, she grabbed her throat and with a raspy voice said, "There's one stuck in my throat."

I prayed out loud, "God, please send Your angels to dig this spirit out of her throat."

Out of the corner of my left eye, I saw a bluish light rush in, going straight for the woman's throat. Immediately, she grabbed her throat, coughed and vomited, and the spirit came out.

Another time, I was praying for a woman who believed that she had a huge serpent wrapped around her body. I asked God to send angels to help us.

After we cast the demons out, the woman asked me, "What are angels?" She was a brand-new convert and had never heard of angels.

"They are spirits," I said, "sent by God to help us. Why?"

"Well," she said, "when you mentioned angels, suddenly the room was filled with bright lights. They looked like tiny spinning wheels of light. I saw a big one sitting on that blue book over there." She was pointing to my Bible with its blue cover.

On another occasion, a Buddhist friend came to church for the first time. I had been inviting him for more than a year, and he finally came. After the service, I went over to greet him and noticed that his eyes were wide open.

"What is that?" he asked. "Do you have special lighting effects? I saw a big column of light behind and to your left as you were speaking. The light was so bright, I couldn't open my eyes."

"No," I said. "That's just the angel of the church protecting the word."

ANGELS NOW AND IN THE FUTURE

When the apostles were thrown into prison for preaching the gospel and healing the sick, an angel appeared and opened the prison doors. (See Acts 5:19.) An angel appeared before Cornelius and instructed him to send men to Joppa to call Peter. (See Acts 10:3–5.) An angel struck King Herod dead when he refused to give God the glory. (See Acts 12:23.) An angel of the Lord rescued Peter, broke through his chains, and let him out of prison. (See Acts 12:7–10.) Angels do superhuman feats to protect us; they accompany us on trips, protect us from the evil one, and stand guard around us.

Angels do countless things for us without our knowledge. A member of my church was driving home up a very steep hill late at night when she blacked out. The next thing she knew she was hanging upside down by her seat belt. She had driven into a ditch and up a hill, and had rolled over onto the car's roof. The vehicle was almost totally demolished. The woman, however, didn't suffer so much as a scratch. Could it be that her angels protected her? I believe so.

Once, I blessed a house where the occupants were used to seeing dark shadows and hearing footsteps on the stairway. I asked God to send angels to stand guard in the house. Six months later, I saw the husband of the family and asked him if he had experienced any strange things after we blessed his house.

"No," he said, "but once I saw a real bright light, like a column of light on my stairway."

The angels were at work.

I believe that in the coming battles against the kingdom of darkness, God will send His many angels to deliver messages to us, to protect us, and to minister in many other ways to the heirs of salvation. (See Hebrews 1:14.) They will work with us for the advancement of the kingdom.

JOY AND LAUGHTER IN FIJI

When I was in Fiji several years ago, our ministry had just emerged from a major battle with the enemy during which God delivered more than one hundred people. As we praised and worshipped the Lord the next morning, some of the students began to fall on the ground, laughing. Others just stood, giggling uncontrollably. Soon, other students were running outside in the yard, stumbling around laughing and giggling. This went on for two hours.

Angels

Later, fifteen students came up to me to share what they experienced. Almost all of them reported seeing hundreds of angels streaming into the room, dancing and laughing with the students. Many who had run around the yard reported playing a form of the child's game of tag with the angels. Another student reported that an angel said that they would return that evening. Sure enough, as soon as we started singing and praising that evening, a shaft of light came down from heaven and filled the room, and hundreds of angels returned to play with the students. They laughed until one o'clock in the morning.

In the days that followed, the laughter did not return, but we were often aware of angels among us, and the anointing was heavy to do the Lord's work.

What the church needs to learn is how to react positively to God's angels, how to cooperate with them, how to ask God for them, and how to join them in spiritual warfare. One thing is certain: angels are everywhere that the saints are.

Eventually, I became so used to having angels around me while ministering in Fiji that I was disappointed when, on one of my last trips, no one saw any angels.

"Gee, Lord," I prayed. "Are You upset with me? Am I doing something wrong this time?"

Nothing happened. However, as we were standing around at the airport in Nadi waiting for our flight home, one of the women talking to me suddenly jumped back, her face flushed.

"My," she said in a hushed voice, "I just saw a huge angel standing behind you. He is so huge that my head comes only up to his thigh!"

I think it was God's way of saying, "As you mature, you need to move by faith and not by sight. Just because you don't see angels doesn't mean that they are not around, protecting you and fighting spiritual battles."

GIVING SKILL AND UNDERSTANDING

In the book of Daniel, God sent the angel Gabriel to Daniel to interpret his vision. Gabriel said, *"O Daniel, I have now come forth to give you skill to understand"* (Daniel 9:22). Apparently, angels can give humankind skill and understanding. It is difficult to say how angels do this, but it is definite that God sent forth the angel. In verse 23, the angel said to Daniel, *"At the beginning of your supplications the command went out."* God will command His angels to help the saints and give skill and understanding. We are never to worship angels, but we *are* to work with them and even ask God to send them to help us.

SERAPHIM: SPINNING ANGELS OF LIGHT

In Scripture, Ezekiel talked about seraphim. (See Ezekiel 1–2.) Seraphim are a type of angel. According to Ezekiel, they flew back and forth with spinning wheels. We know that angels—multitudes upon multitudes of angels—surround God's throne where they minister to God:

> *Then I looked, and I heard the voice of many angels around the throne, the living creatures, and the elders; and the number of them was ten thousand times ten thousand, and thousands of thousands.* (Revelation 5:11)

References to these servants of God fill the New Testament. Jesus spoke often of angels. (See, for example, Matthew 13:39, 41, 49; 16:27; 18:10; 22:30; and 24:31.) If there were no such things as angels, that would make God a liar. Jesus mentioned angels when he told Nathanael, *"Most assuredly, I say to you, here-after you shall see heaven open, and the angels of God ascending and descending upon the Son of Man"* (John 1:51). That announcement was not just for Jesus' day; it is for today as well. Angels still ascend and descend upon the children of light.

An angel also ministered to Jesus in the garden of Gethse-mane before His crucifixion. (See Luke 22:43.) When Jesus rose from the dead, an angel sat on the stone that had been rolled back and spoke to the women who had come to the tomb. (See Matthew 28:2.)

When Jesus ascended into heaven, two angels appeared and said to the disciples, *"Men of Galilee, why do you stand gazing up into heaven? This same Jesus, who was taken up from you into heaven, will so come in like manner as you saw Him go into heaven"* (Acts 1:11).

Just as He has done in the past, God will send His many angels to help His elect in the end times ahead.

ANGELS WILL EXECUTE JUDGMENT

The book of Revelation says that angels will play a major role in carrying out God's judgments on the earth in the end times. In Revelation 7, God calls four angels to carry out His judgments: *"And he cried with a loud voice to the four angels to whom it was granted to harm the earth and the sea"* (Revelation 7:2). In Revelation 9:15, angels slay one-third of all men. Angels with seven plagues carry out judgment on the earth in Revelation 15:8. In Revelation 16:4, vials are poured by angels upon the sea. Every living creature in the sea dies. Different vials bring additional judgments. God's angels will carry out His will during the tribulation period to come.

The point is: angels will play a major role in the end times soon to come. They are already on assignment from God and are all over the earth. There will come a time when the true saints of God will know these angels and work side by side with them.

When we go against the kingdom of darkness, we are not alone. There are multitudes of angels surrounding us and standing ready to do battle for us. It is as if the angels are anxious to get into battle. They are just waiting for us to do our part.

OF VARIOUS SIZES AND APPEARANCES

God created the angels. Apparently, they come in different sizes and shapes. The Bible calls some seraphim and some cherubim. Some have more than one pair of wings; some have heads of animals and feathers. (See Ezekiel 1:5–10.)

> When we go against the kingdom of darkness, we are not alone. There are multitudes of angels surrounding us, ready to do battle for us.

Angels can appear as huge human beings, often eight to ten feet tall and powerfully built. Warring angels have been seen in full armor and carrying swords. They look like weight lifters and are beautiful and awesome to behold. Some have wings and some do not. They can also appear as everyday human beings—not beautiful, but ordinary. Hebrews 13:2 says, *"Do not forget to entertain strangers, for by so doing some have unwittingly entertained angels."*

Angels

Once, I parked my car on the street, waiting with my wife and two young sons to pick up my older son and daughter from language school. It was hot, and we were perspiring in the car. As we sat there, I noticed an ice cream shop nearby and hatched an idea.

"It's too hot. Let's buy some ice cream," I exclaimed.

My wife replied, "But I don't have any money, I was too busy to go to the bank."

I had no money either. We sat there for a few minutes, disappointed at the prospect of going without ice cream. All of a sudden, an old Asian man shuffled up out of nowhere from behind the car. He started peering into my car, waving at my two young sons, and smiling at them like a kindly old grandfather playing with his grandsons.

He came up to my wife's open window and said, "It's my birthday. Let me buy you some ice cream so we can celebrate. Is that okay?"

My wife and I looked at each other, and my older son said, "Can we, Dad?"

"I guess so," I said, "but only for the kids." I was too proud and embarrassed to accept ice cream from a stranger.

We watched the man as he bought two ice cream cones and handed them to my son. Then he dug into his pocket, put something into my son's hand and pointed to the sky. My son walked back to the car.

"Dad," my son said, "he gave me this, and he told me to get some ice cream for you and Mom, too." It was a ten-dollar bill. Then my son said, "Just before he left, the man pointed to the sky and said, 'Tell your parents I came from up there.' He pointed to the sky, and then he walked away."

Excitedly, I told my son, "Run, see if you can find him and thank him."

My son ran around the building where the old man had walked. He could not have walked more than fifty feet since he walked very slowly.

My son soon came back and exclaimed, "He's gone! I don't know where he is."

If the man had walked around the building, he would have been in clear sight. He simply disappeared. I believe he was an angel. How wonderful is our God! I hadn't even prayed that He would send an angel to give us ice cream. I never ate better ice cream in my life.

WE DO NOT COMMAND ANGELS

Angels are ministering spirits to the heirs of salvation. We do not command them; God sends them to help us. They obey God and do not obey men directly. Psalm 103:20 says, *"Bless the LORD, you His angels, who excel in strength, who do His word, heeding the voice of His word."*

We enlist the help of angels by asking God to send them. God is faithful in sending angels to us if it is His will. I say "if it is His will" because there may be times when a human is working against the will of God, either intentionally or unintentionally, and it is inconceivable that His angels would carry out any tasks that are contrary to His will.

Often, God sends His angels without our asking. It is highly probable that angels have protected and saved us from many of Satan's snares without us even knowing it. Doubtless, your angels have protected you without you even knowing it.

Just imagine all the misfortunes and accidents set up by Satan that have been repeatedly thwarted and diverted by God's angels on our behalf.

CORPORATE ANGEL WARFARE

When God's people get together and wage war corporately against Satan's kingdom, so do God's angels. As we bind up the strongmen and attack the mid-heavens, angels take our words and execute them.

At a prayer retreat, the men of our church gathered to conduct spiritual warfare. About fifteen of us stood, prayed, and shouted as we bound up the ruling spirits in the heavens. As we continued hurling spears of prayer and attacking the demonic realm, several men saw a multitude of angels doing battle, lined up in perfect formation. Others saw chariots pulled by huge white horses.

> It is highly probable that angels have protected and saved us from many of Satan's snares without us even knowing it.

As the saints hurled spears of prayer, men witnessed angels taking the spears in the spirit and giving them such tremendous force and impetus that they smashed through and created a hole through which the brilliant light of heaven burst.

One man saw a huge demonic spirit dressed in green and looking like a Chinese warrior spirit named Kwan Dai Goong. He was peering down at the group as if to say, "What's going on here? You people think you can defeat us?

No way." The spirit was surprised that a group of humans could even penetrate into the mid-heavens.

Unfortunately, the men did not continue the warfare thereafter. It is my belief that if God's people would conduct spiritual warfare on a daily or even weekly basis, we would bind the strongmen and reclaim our cities, towns, and neighborhoods for the kingdom of God. Nevertheless, God's angels are always ready to do battle for the saints.

WAITING FOR GOD'S COMMAND

On a trip to Fiji, four girls testified that one evening they were all taken up to heaven in the spirit. An angel took one girl to see an enormous golden chariot filled with hundreds of angels in full battle uniform. At the head of the chariot was a huge angel, sword drawn and raised to the sky. He stood so perfectly still she thought it was a statue. However, when she stood to the side of the angel, his eyes glanced down at her, and she realized that he was real.

"What is he doing?" the girl asked the angel.

"He's waiting for the command to go forward," her angel guide replied.

One day soon, there is going to be a colossal battle pitting Michael and the rest of God's angels against Satan and his evil horde. On that glorious day, Satan and his fellow rebel angels will be defeated and cast down to earth.

Revelation 12:7–9 says:

And war broke out in heaven: Michael and his angels fought with the dragon; and the dragon and his angels fought, but they did not prevail, nor was a place found for them in heaven any longer. So the great dragon was cast out, that serpent of old, called the Devil and Satan, who deceives the whole world; he was cast to the earth, and his angels were cast out with him.

Michael and his angels will fight against the dragon and his angels because the saints on earth will be fighting too. It is improbable that God would summarily command Michael to do the saints a favor by clearing the heavens without the saints engaging in the battle as well.

Remember Jesus' words as He gave Paul his mission on the road to Damascus: *"I will deliver you from the Jewish people, as well as from the Gentiles, to whom I now send you, to open their eyes, in order to turn them from darkness to light, and from the power of Satan to God"* (Acts 26:17–18). It is still our mission today: to push back the darkness and confront the power of Satan.

When the saints realize that they need to come together to engage the enemy and start crying out and warring in the mid-heavens, Michael and his angels will take the prayers of the saints and fulfill them.

As Jesus said,

But if I cast out demons by the Spirit of God, surely the king-dom of God has come upon you. Or how can one enter a strong man's house and plunder his goods, unless he first binds the strong man? And then he will plunder his house.

(Matthew 12:28–29)

As the church does battle against the strongmen in the heavenlies and prays to bind them up, the angels of God will take chains from heaven and do the job for us. One day, when the body of Christ unites in battle, God will send the arch-angel, Michael, and His angels to defeat the entire satanic army in the mid-heavens and cast them down to earth. God is gathering His troops right now.

> Scripture makes it clear that we are not to worship angels in any way. They are merely fellow created servants of the most high God.

I believe that there are multitudes of angels in the heavenlies poised for battle. When the body of Christ becomes mature enough to engage the enemy in all-out battle, the angels of God will fight for us and with us—side by side. When Jesus comes back, He will return with help: *"And the armies in heaven, clothed in fine linen, white and clean, followed Him on white horses"* (Revelation 19:14). Notice that He is accompanied by *armies*—plural. One of the groups we know will be available will be men and women of earth:

> *They sang as it were a new song before the throne...and no one could learn that song except the hundred and forty-four thousand who were redeemed from the earth.*
> (Revelation 14:3)

I believe one of those armies will be that hundred and forty-four thousand men and women redeemed from the earth. I believe the other army will be made up of angels.

Scripture makes it clear that we are not to worship angels in any way. (See Colossians 2:18.) They are merely fellow created servants of the most high God. On the other hand, we need to realize that we are not alone. An entire army of angels is on our side as we mature in Christ. There will come a day when seeing angels will be a commonplace event for the true saints of God. It is inevitable that the saints will one day play a part in defeating Satan's kingdom with God's angels working side by side.

Angels will play a major role in those end times. Those who are walking with the Lord and working for the kingdom will labor with angels to accomplish the Lord's will. Angels are therefore our fellow laborers.

PART II

GLOBAL SPIRITUAL CONFLICT

CHAPTER SIX

WE ARE IN A WAR!

Spiritual warfare is far more than just casting out a few devils, healing the sick, jumping up and down, or cleansing haunted houses.

For we do not wrestle against flesh and blood, but against principalities, against powers, against the rulers of the darkness of this age, against spiritual hosts of wickedness in the heavenly places. (Ephesians 6:12)

We know that we are of God, and the whole world lies under the sway of the wicked one. (1 John 5:19)

Our duty is not limited to freeing a few people here and there. It is much broader. We are in the middle of a conflict between God's kingdom of light and Satan's kingdom of darkness.

THE GREATEST REVIVAL OF ALL TIME

In Matthew, Jesus said, *"And this gospel of the kingdom will be preached in all the world as a witness to all the nations, and **then the end will come"** (Matthew 24:14, emphasis added).

In Mark, Jesus spoke of the end of the world to come:

These are the beginnings of sorrows. But watch out for yourselves, for they will deliver you up to councils, and you will be beaten in the synagogues. You will be brought before rulers and kings for My sake, for a testimony to them. And the gospel must first be preached to all the nations.

(Mark 13:8–10)

Likewise, Revelation 14:6 says,

Then I saw another angel flying in the midst of heaven, having the everlasting gospel to preach to those who dwell on the earth; to every nation, tribe, tongue, and people.

In other words, before the end of the world comes, there will first be a great revival! The Word of God will not come back void!

A VISION AND AN ANGEL

In 1998, I was teaching at a Bible college in the remote town of Lal-lo, in the Cagayan province of the northern Philippines. I asked the students to come forward so I could baptize them in the Holy Spirit. When I laid my hands on two girls to my right, all sixteen students fell to the ground at once and began weeping and speaking in tongues.

At the same time, my niece was standing in the middle of the church and had a vision of a huge rice field stretching out as far as the eyes could see. The stalks were still green, but so laden with grain that they almost touched the ground. The rice grains turned into people dressed in white robes. She felt the presence of God and saw a huge angel standing behind me, a large scroll in his hands.

"Are you the angel of this church?" she asked.

"No," the angel replied. "I'm the angel of Tucalana," referring to a local neighborhood district. "This scroll contains the names of all the men, women, and children that will be coming into the kingdom of our Lord Jesus Christ in the upcoming revival."

All the time, my niece was seeing many smaller angels flying beneath the high ceiling.

REVIVAL IN THE PHILIPPINES

On my return to Hawaii, I learned that many prophets had prophesied that the last revival would start in the Philippines. American James Horvath produced a video tape message in which he received a vision of the map of the Philippines. On that map, a red ball bounced from north to south, from east to west, starting fires wherever it landed. Then it leaped to other countries. Since that time, Horvath has been coming to the Philippines every year to conduct large crusade meetings in the northern provinces.

Three years later, in early 2001, we returned to Lal-lo where my wife and two other women saw the same angel standing behind me during a deliverance service. This time, two large angels stood on each side of him. He is waiting for God's command to go forward. Revival is coming to the Philippines!

I'm well aware that other prophets have claimed that the final revival will begin in other places around the world. Where it begins is not really important; the important thing is that God's will be done and that the body of Christ prays together and fights the kingdom of darkness as one body. Only then will we usher in the coming revival.

However, revival will not be automatic. What does revival require from the body of Christ? What must precede harvest? These are important questions.

FASTING AND PRAYER IS NOT ENOUGH

Many Christians around the world fast and pray constantly for revival. However, revival will not come so easily this time because the last revival of this age will be different from all previous ones.

> Sparking the next revival will be far more difficult for it will be infinitely larger in both length and scope. It will also be the last and greatest of this age.

Scholars claim that past revivals took place because of the fervent prayers of a few dedicated and determined men and women. Evan Roberts led a group in prayer for seven years before revival came to Wales in 1904. William Seymour and Frank Bartleman fasted and prayed so long and hard that their wives feared for their lives. However, they moved the hand of God and revival ignited in a tiny church on Azusa Street in Los Angeles in 1906. Charles Finney and others fasted and prayed and the Second Great Awakening took place in the early 1800s.

Sparking the next revival will be far more difficult for it will be infinitely larger in both length and scope. It will also be the last and greatest revival of this age. The Great Welsh Revival lasted only one year (1904–1905) and drew somewhere between 100 and 180 thousand new converts. The Second

Great Awakening of Charles Finney brought in 500 thousand new converts. The Azusa Street Revival involved similar figures, although later it was credited with helping to spread Pentecostalism around the world.

The coming revival, however, will involve hundreds of millions of converts around the world! Truly, *"this gospel of the kingdom **will be preached in all the world** as a witness to all the nations"* (Matthew 24:14, emphasis added).

This coming revival also marks the end of Satan's reign on earth. In the past, Satan could afford to lose a few hundred thousand souls as long as his reign as the god of this world was not seriously threatened. This time around, however, Revelation tells us that Satan will be defeated and cast down to earth, never to return to the heavens. Even now, Satan knows his ultimate fate.

Satan still rules as *"the prince of the power of the air"* (Ephesians 2:2). Nevertheless, his defeat is ordained. (See Luke 10:18; Revelation 12:7–10.) In the meantime, he still goes to the throne of God to accuse us day and night.

SATAN'S LAST STAND

Satan is not going to take his demise lying down. Even as revival comes, he will not quit. He will move against all churches and Christians with vengeance and great wrath. (See Revelation 12:13–17.) He will establish his worldwide government and religion (see Revelation 13:7–8, 11–18) to rule the world and destroy Christianity.

Satan's beast is going *"to make war with the saints...to overcome them"* (Revelation 13:7). Daniel put it this way: *"I was watching; and the same horn* [on the beast] *was making war against the saints, and prevailing against them"* (Daniel 7:21).

The description continues:

He shall speak pompous words against the Most High, shall persecute the saints of the Most High, and shall intend to change times and law. Then the saints shall be given into his hand for a time and times and half a time.

(Daniel 7:25)

For three and a half years, Satan is going to attempt to destroy the church and the saints. There is definitely a war coming!

WORLDWIDE RELIGIONS AND GOVERNMENT

Revelation describes the world events leading up to this war: *"And authority was given him over every tribe, tongue, and nation. All who dwell on the earth will worship him, whose names have not been written in the Book of Life"* (Revelation 13:7–8).

Most Bible scholars refer to this world leader as the "Dictator Beast" or "Antichrist." In verses 11–18, it says that a second beast will give power to the first beast. In describing this second beast, it says, *"He had two horns like a lamb and spoke like a dragon"* (verse 11). In other words, he will appear as the representative of the Lamb of God, or Christ on earth, but will actually work for Satan. Revelation 19:20 calls him the *"false prophet."* In all probability, he will be a religious figure recognized as a world leader of "Christianity."

On August 30, 2000, over one thousand delegates of every major (and many minor) religion in the world met in the General Assembly Chambers of the United Nations in an attempt to form a charter for what would be a one-world religion. All religions were widely cheered except Christianity. According to Dave Hunt's book, *Global Peace*, every two years since 1986 the Vatican has invited representatives of other major religions to attend meetings to discuss and promote a one-world religion.[8]

On September 3, 2000, delegates from over one hundred forty countries met in the same UN chambers to gain consensus for the Charter for Global Democracy, which would, in effect, transform the United Nations into a one-world government.

THE COMING REVIVAL

Most of the world's past revivals have been sporadic and limited in scope; and, of course, none of them marked the end of the world. According to the Bible, however, the coming revival will bring unprecedented persecution and tribulation, and it will be the beginning of the end of the world as we know it.

According to Scripture, Satan is well aware of the fact that he is doomed to be bound, thrown into a bottomless pit (see Revelation 20:2–3), and ultimately cast into the Lake of Fire. (See Revelation 20:10.) In light of that, Satan is determined to destroy every Christian on the face of the earth. Do not let yourself become deceived. The war has already begun!

CHRISTIANITY OUTLAWED

In Matthew, Jesus' disciples asked Him about signs of the end times: *"Tell us, when will these things be? And what will be the sign of Your coming, and of the end of the age?"* (Matthew 24:3).

After detailing the events marking the *"beginning of sorrows"* (verse 8), Jesus said,

And this gospel of the kingdom will be preached in all the world as a witness to all the nations, and then the end will come. (Matthew 24:14)

Before the end comes, every person will hear of Jesus and have the opportunity to accept Him as Lord and Savior. Many will accept this invitation. Others will not.

Sadly, in the next verse, Jesus said, *"Therefore when you see the 'abomination of desolation,' spoken of by Daniel the prophet, standing in the holy place"* (whoever reads, let him understand), *"then let those who are in Judea flee to the mountains"* (Matthew 24:15–16).

Just what is the *"abomination of desolation spoken of by Daniel the prophet"*? Let's look at what Daniel said:

*He even exalted himself as high as the Prince of the host; and by him **the daily sacrifices were taken away,** and **the place of His sanctuary was cast down.** Because of transgression, an army was given over to the horn to oppose the daily sacrifices; and he cast truth down to the ground. He did all this and prospered. Then I heard a holy one speaking; and another holy one said to that certain one who was speaking, "How long will the vision be, concerning the daily sacrifices and the transgression of desolation, the giving of both the sanctuary and the host to be trampled under foot?" And he said to me, "**For two thousand three hundred days**; then the sanctuary shall be cleansed."* (Daniel 8:11–14, emphasis added)

Worship of Jesus will be declared illegal. All church buildings and sanctuaries will be destroyed or taken away and Christians will be arrested or killed for twenty-three hundred days—roughly six and one-third years. All of this persecution will begin as revival breaks out in various parts of the world. An army will initiate military action against the church.

In some areas of the world, this has already begun. In China, true Christianity has been illegal for over fifty years. The Communist government has destroyed church buildings and continues to incarcerate or kill "unauthorized" Christians. "Authorized" Christianity is the government-sanctioned Three-Self Church, which is more concerned with patriotism than true faith. To find the true church of Jesus Christ, you have to go underground.[9]

> While the body of Christ eagerly anticipates revival and harvest, it is ill-prepared for the spiritual war and persecution that will accompany it.

Unfortunately, while the body of Christ eagerly anticipates revival and harvest, it is ill-prepared for the spiritual war and physical persecution that will accompany it.

THE GREAT DECEPTION

Ordinary fasting and praying will not spark the coming revival. Demonic powers are gathering strength and implementing Satan's nefarious plans. Satan is determined to prevent revival and a big part of that plan is deception.

Jesus warned us that there would be great deception in the end times:

Then many false prophets will rise up and deceive many.
(Matthew 24:11)

For false christs and false prophets will rise and show great signs and wonders to deceive, if possible, even the elect.
(Matthew 24:24)

Deception is dangerous. It will lead many astray, causing them to be unprepared, immature, divided, and thinking only of their own peace and prosperity—not knowing that destruction is almost upon them. Because of their backsliding, God Himself will allow some to fall into the trap of deception.

That's what happened in the days of the prophet Jeremiah. Because God's people rejected His warnings and refused to go back to His true ways, God allowed His rebellious people to be deceived. Jeremiah then declared,

Ah, Lord GOD! Surely You have greatly deceived this people and Jerusalem, saying, "You shall have peace," whereas the sword reaches to the heart. (Jeremiah 4:10)

Can the majority of God's people become deceived? History and Scripture would say they can.

Satan is the father of lies. (See John 8:44.) He has already brainwashed some members of the body of Christ to the point that many do not believe that there is such thing as the devil. To them, Satan is merely a symbolic personification of evil in the world. Others do not believe that the Holy Spirit is on earth. Still others do not believe that Christians can have demons. They are deceived.

If they were around today, first-century Christians would have a hard time recognizing much of the Christianity they suffered and bled to establish. The early church met in circles, not in rows facing the professional preacher in the front.

There was little of the ritual, pageantry, and ceremony you find today. When they met, the Holy Spirit moved, people spoke and sang in tongues, the sick and lame were healed, and peoples' needs were met. Over the years and centuries, Satan has corrupted significant portions of the body of Christ, leading them away from truth and into deception. Instead of allowing the Holy Spirit to lead, people instituted rituals, man-made celebrations, customs, and traditions, leaving little resemblance to the beauty and simplicity of the early church.

From time to time, the Barna Research Group conducts surveys on the current attitudes and beliefs of the church in America. These are some of the results of their 1997 survey:

1) 34 percent of born-again Christians, 53 percent of *all* Christians, and 73 percent of mainline Protestants **believe that if a person is good, he will go to heaven**. You do not need Jesus to go to heaven.

2) 66 percent of evangelicals **don't believe that the Bible is totally accurate**; 74 percent of Catholics and 42 percent of *all* Christians agree.

3) 28 percent of born-again Christians, 65 percent of evangelicals, and 40 percent of *all* Christians **believe that Jesus was a sinner when He walked the earth**.

4) 52 percent of born-again Christians, 72 percent of Catholics, and 80 percent of *all* Christians **don't believe that the devil is real, that he is only a symbol of evil**.

5) 55 percent of born-again Christians and 61 percent of *all* Christians **don't believe that the Holy Spirit is a person, only a symbol of God's presence and power**.

6) 35% of born-again Christians and 39% of all Christians **do not believe that Jesus rose from the dead bodily**. (Emphasis added.)[10]

BLASPHEMY ABOUNDS

Some modern Christian "beliefs" are pure blasphemies that no longer follow the Bible or the ways of God. Prominent religious leaders have joined "ecumenical" movements claiming that you don't have to know Jesus to get to heaven—just live a "good life." They question the authority and accuracy of Scripture. Many are endorsing and performing same-sex marriages. Some denominations are even ordaining openly homosexual clergy. And these are church leaders! Will you join them, or warn them?

This is a crucial question. Beware of allowing politically correct lies to seep into the church where they can compromise the truth in any way, even for those you love.

THE ECUMENICAL MOVEMENT

As mentioned earlier, the Bible says that a person who claims to be Christ's representative on earth will lead the one-world religion. This leader, however, will actually work for the devil.

When I was in Colorado a few years ago, the *Aspen Times* published a front-page letter from the Vatican to all Roman Catholics encouraging them to welcome "our Buddhist brothers," indicating that there was much that we can learn about God from them.

It was Pope John Paul II who went to the United Nations to encourage a one-world government and greatly influenced the forming of the European Union. The first meeting of the European Union was at the Vatican.

We Are in a War

The Bible makes clear what awaits those who resist the beast:

> *Then I saw the souls of those who had been beheaded for their witness to Jesus and for the word of God, who had not worshiped the beast or his image, and had not received his mark on their foreheads or on their hands.*
>
> (Revelation 20:4)

Radical Islamists are already beheading "infidels"—anyone who does not acknowledge and obey Allah or his prophet, Muhammad. Islam will soon become the dominant religion in Europe, the home of the Roman Catholic Church.

A Warning from God

The apostle Paul clearly warned us about introducing another Jesus or new doctrines:

> *But I fear….if he who comes preaches **another Jesus** whom we have not preached, or if you receive **a different spirit** which you have not received, or **a different gospel** which you have not accepted; you may well put up with it!*
>
> (2 Corinthians 11:3-4, emphasis added)

There are many "Jesuses" out there other than the Jesus of the Bible. If the Jesus being worshipped at your church is not the same one found in the pages of the Bible, then it is a false Jesus.

Catholicism promotes a Jesus so wrathful that you cannot go to God directly. You must go through the "saints," or through His mother, Mary. Scripture, however, is clear on the point that Jesus is our only mediator: *"There is one God and one mediator between God and men, the Man Christ Jesus"*

(1 Timothy 2:5). The Bible says that we can enter boldly into His presence by the blood of Jesus (see Hebrews 10:19), and nothing can separate us from His love. (See Romans 8:38–39.)

The Jehovah's Witnesses have a Jesus who was merely a man and not God, but because of his great works, Jehovah the almighty God made him into a lesser God. They claim that Jesus was actually only Michael, the archangel. Mormons worship a Jesus who has a brother by the name of Lucifer.

These are not the same Jesus described in the Bible. The only two infallible sources of truth are the Bible and the Holy Spirit. They will never contradict each other.

"You worship what you do not know….The true worshipers will worship the Father in spirit and truth; for the Father is seeking such to worship Him" (John 4:22–23).

Despite the warnings not to accept any other Jesus or added doctrines not taught by the early apostles, the body of Christ has embraced many doctrines never taught by the early apostles. Catholics as well as Protestants have disregarded and violated Bible warnings.

Paul was emphatic in Galatians 1:8–9:

But even if we, or an angel from heaven, preach any other gospel to you than what we have preached to you, let him be accursed.

Paul once again warned us of doctrines not taught by the first apostles.

I charge you therefore before God and the Lord Jesus Christ….Preach the word! Be ready in season and out *of season. **Convince, rebuke, exhort,** with all longsuffering and teaching. For the time will come when they will not endure sound doctrine, but according to their own desires, because they have itching ears, they will heap up for themselves teachers; and they will turn their ears away from the truth, and be turned aside to fables.*

(2 Timothy 4:1-4, emphasis added)

Jude 3 urges believers to *"contend earnestly for the faith which was once for all delivered to the saints."* If the original apostles did not teach it, do not believe it, no matter how good it seems. Do not add to, subtract from, or modify the truths of the Bible in order to please men. (See also Titus 1:9-11, 13; 2 Thessalonians 3:6, 14-15.)

Because we have not guarded the truth, many new doctrines and practices have entered the body of Christ. Like an insidious cancer that first goes undetected as it spreads ever so slowly, these doctrines have eaten away at the gospel. As a result, the church is no longer the bastion of truth that God intended it to be, *"The house of God, which is the church of the living God, the pillar and ground of the truth"* (1 Timothy 3:15). We have fallen away from the church's early beliefs and doctrines and substituted man's philosophies, customs, and ideas.

> Do not add to, subtract from, or modify the truths of the Bible in order to please men.

As Paul stated, *"Let no one deceive you by any means; for that Day* [the return of Jesus] *will not come unless the falling away comes first"* (2 Thessalonians 2:3). Instead of *"falling away,"*

The Amplified Bible uses the word *apostasy*, which means, "to turn away from one's original beliefs." Before the end of the world, many Christians will fall away from the faith.

Jesus said, *"I am the way, the truth, and the life"* (John 14:6). The only true Jesus is the Jesus of the Bible, and the only true doctrines are those taught by the original apostles.

The love of truth will soon become very costly indeed.

COMPROMISING THE GOSPEL

In 1995, I went to Fiji and met four girls who were "slain in the Spirit" for six hours at a church service one night. Afterward, I interviewed and videotaped them. All claimed that two angels accompanied each of them to heaven where they saw many things. Then, the angels took them to hell. To their shock and surprise, they saw a great many pastors there.

"Why are they here?" they asked the angel with them.

"Because they compromised the gospel," was the angel's reply.

At the end of the interview, I asked one of the girls for a last word she could share with the Christians in America. With tears, she said, "Tell them not to compromise the gospel. They will go to hell!"

Is "unity" with other religions more important than the truth? Has Christianity become a social philosophy that is so embarrassed over its message of uncompromising truth that it chooses instead to water down the gospel? Is it an embarrassment to claim that no one can go to the Father except through Jesus? Is the truth worth fighting for, or is it better to compromise the gospel for the sake of social and political correctness and "peace and brotherhood"? After all, Jesus said,

> *Do not think that I came to bring peace on earth. I did not come to bring peace but a sword. For I have come to "set a man against his father, a daughter against her mother, and a daughter-in-law against her mother-in-law"; and "a man's enemies will be those of his own household." He who loves father or mother more than Me is not worthy of Me. And he who loves son or daughter more than Me is not worthy of Me.* (Matthew 10:34–37)

THE TRUE GOSPEL OF THE KINGDOM

Today, many preachers share a salvation message that promises, "Become a Christian, and God will bless you. You will have everything you ever wanted. You will live at the top!"

In the days of the early church, the only true gospel of salvation was that of the cross of Jesus. The apostle Paul wrote:

> *Jews request a sign, and Greeks seek after wisdom; but we preach Christ crucified, to the Jews a stumbling block and to the Greeks foolishness, but to those who are called, both Jews and Greeks, Christ the power of God and the wisdom of God.* (1 Corinthians 1:22–24)

Author and teacher John MacArthur points out that the word *foolishness* is the same Greek word from which we get the word *moron*.[11] To the world, the gospel message seemed to be a ridiculous and even "moronic." The true gospel of salvation is the cross! Paul wrote,

> *And I, brethren, when I came to you, did not come with excellence of speech or of wisdom declaring to you the testimony*

of God. For I determined not to know anything among you except Jesus Christ and Him crucified. I was with you in weakness, in fear, and in much trembling. And my speech and my preaching were not with persuasive words of human wisdom, but in demonstration of the Spirit and of power, that your faith should not be in the wisdom of men but in the power of God. (1 Corinthians 2:1–5)

Paul was a man with a great ability to preach and teach. He was wise and eloquent. Why would he have fear and trembling, and why did he avoid enticing words of man's wisdom? The answer: he feared that he would somehow compromise the message of the cross. To Paul, there was nothing worse than this. He was exceedingly careful not to preach anything other than the cross when speaking to unbelievers.

> Just because a church draws in tens of thousands of people does not mean that it is free of deception.

Today, pastors freely draw people into their churches with the enticing words of man's wisdom, rejecting the message of the cross and repentance in favor of the promises of blessings and prosperity for anyone who becomes a Christian. In a nationally televised interview, one prominent mega-church pastor said that his church would never talk about negative things such as sin, the cross, or blood. Just because a church draws in tens of thousands of people does not mean that it is free of deception.

When Jesus' disciples asked Him why He spoke plainly to them but in parables to other people, He answered, *"Because it has been given to you to know the mysteries of the kingdom of heaven, but to them it has not been given....Because seeing they do not see, and hearing they do not hear, nor do they understand"* (Matthew 13:11, 13).

It is the Holy Spirit who opens the ears and hearts of the people to understand and accept salvation. It is the message of the cross that separates those who would choose God from those who do not. It is the Holy Spirit who convicts the hearts of men so that they might be saved. It is *not* any enticing message given by men.

The seemingly foolish message of the cross, given by lowly men, is the power of God unto salvation. (See 1 Corinthians 1:18.) It is the message of the cross, received by men, that brings salvation, not a message of blessing and prosperity. *"It pleased God through the foolishness of the message preached to save those who believe"* (1 Corinthians 1:21). God has rejected enticing messages and promises of a good life *"that no flesh should glory in His presence"* (verse 29), that no man can say that by his clever arguments he saved anyone. That is why, despite all his brilliance and impeccable qualifications, the apostle Paul said, *"But God forbid that I should boast except in the cross of our Lord Jesus Christ, by whom the world has been crucified to me, and I to the world"* (Galatians 6:14).

To say that God will bless you if you accept Jesus in some quid pro quo fashion runs contrary to what Jesus taught. Indeed, Jesus said that if a man or woman would follow Him, his own family and friends may become his adversaries (see Matthew 10:34–37) and that they must carry their cross daily. (See verse 38.) A follower of Jesus may lose his or her family, friends, business, and even his or her very life as a result.

The true gospel message is that, while salvation is free, being a true disciple of Jesus will cost you much. The ticket to heaven is exceedingly precious and one should be willing to pay any price for it. Jesus said,

Again, the kingdom of heaven is like treasure hidden in a field, which a man found and hid; and for joy over it he goes and sells all that he has and buys that field. Again, the kingdom of heaven is like a merchant seeking beautiful pearls, who, when he had found one pearl of great price, went and sold all that he had and bought it. (Matthew 13:44–46)

Jesus also said,

Do not lay up for yourselves treasures on earth, where moth and rust destroy and where thieves break in and steal; but lay up for yourselves treasures in heaven, where neither moth nor rust destroys and where thieves do not break in and steal. For where your treasure is, there your heart will be also. (Matthew 6:19–21)

A great deal of the prosperity message we hear today is not only unbiblical; it is straight out of the pit of hell!

THE WAY OF BALAAM

Both Peter and Jude warned against following the way of Balaam—using God's gifts of the Spirit for personal gain and prosperity. (See 2 Peter 2:15.)

Woe to them! For they have gone in the way of Cain, have run greedily in the error of Balaam for profit, and perished in the rebellion of Korah. (Jude 11)

It is important to point out that money is not, on its own, good or bad. Money is merely a tool for man to use and, like any other tool, it can be an instrument of good or evil. It takes money to support a ministry and to share the gospel. It takes money to send missionaries to foreign lands. Jesus had benefactors who gave him money, food, shelter, and even the tomb from which he was resurrected. There are many who misquote Scripture, claiming that "money is the root of all evil." The actual quote reveals the true problem with the way in which we handle our money:

> *Those who desire to be rich fall into temptation and a snare, and into many foolish and harmful lusts which drown men in destruction and perdition.* **For the love of money is a root of all kinds of evil,** *for which some have strayed from the faith in their greediness, and pierced themselves through with many sorrows.*
>
> (1 Timothy 6:9–10, emphasis added)

Too many Christians are in love with money. Too many church leaders have grown rich off their ministry. They compete against one another for the biggest church, the fastest jet, and the largest bank account. They try to outdo each other with thousand-dollar suits and million-dollar mansions. The saints love to hear "uplifting" messages on how to have a better and more prosperous life. They flock to these profitable pastors, hoping that some of that wealth and "blessing" will rub off on them. The church has become just as materialistic, covetous, and compromising as the world—maybe more!

Once again, the situation was similar in Jeremiah's day when God spoke to him about the sorry state of His people, saying,

> *Because from the least of them even to the greatest of them, everyone is given to covetousness; and from the prophet*

even to the priest, everyone deals falsely. They have also healed the hurt of My people slightly, Saying, "Peace, peace!" when there is no peace. Were they ashamed when they had committed abomination? No! They were not at all ashamed; nor did they know how to blush. Therefore they shall fall among those who fall; at the time I punish them, they shall be cast down. (Jeremiah 6:13–15)

According to *Strong's Exhaustive Concordance of the Bible*, one of the definitions of *peace* is "prosperity." Some of these televangelists who say, "Prosperity, prosperity!" are millionaires. They refuse to turn back to God's ways. For them, surrendering your life to God has become passé.

Notice the next verse of the passage in Jeremiah:

Thus says the LORD: "Stand in the ways and see, and ask for the old paths, where the good way is, and walk in it; then you will find rest for your souls." But they said, "We will not walk in it." (verse 16)

Jesus did not come with a prosperity message. When *"a certain scribe came and said to Him, 'Teacher, I will follow You wherever You go'"* (Matthew 8:19), Jesus replied, *"Foxes have holes and birds of the air have nests, but the Son of Man has nowhere to lay His head"* (verse 20). In other words, "If you want to follow Me, don't expect an easy life. You are not promised comfort or possessions; you may not have even a home or bed to sleep in."

Some of those who continue to preach the unadulterated truth—repentance, sacrifice, taking up one's cross—have become unpopular, rejected, and even ostracized. Their congregations may not swell into the thousands. They preach what the saints *need* to hear, not what they *want* to hear. If you don't believe this is true, I once received an invitation from a very large church to attend a seminar to learn how to grow your church. One of the subjects was: "How to take a survey to find out what the people want to hear."

Satan's greatest strategy is to deceive the whole world. Jesus warned repeatedly of great deception in the end times. Unfortunately, the church is already being deceived and is losing the war. Even worse, most of us do not even realize we are in a war!

CHAPTER SEVEN

THE KEY TO REVIVAL: SPIRITUAL WARFARE

I n order to spark revival, the church must not only fast and pray, it must also fight against the kingdom of darkness with every weapon it has. There must be unity, a close relationship with God, spiritual maturity, diligence, love, obedience, and so forth, but is the church does not confront the kingdom of darkness and defeat Satan and his demons, Jesus cannot come back and revival will not come.

BINDING UP THE STRONGMEN

As I explained in my previous book, *Spiritual Warfare*, Satan has assigned ruler spirits (or strongmen) over every country, area, city, village, neighborhood, family, church, and person. The bigger the area or the more dangerous the area to Satan, the more powerful the ruler spirits he assigns to control that area. In the Philippines, he has assigned spirits of deception, idolatry, thievery, corruption, pride, poverty, greed, antichrist, witchcraft, Jezebel and Ahab, slavery, sexual immorality, violence, murder, hatred, anger, religiosity, and so forth. It varies from area to area. You can discern the spirits by their fruits. (See Matthew 7:15–16.)

In many parts of America and Europe, witchcraft predominates, as well as formalism, legalism, and tradition. Hatred, racial discrimination, poverty, and crime also rule over these areas.

In the Middle East, sectarianism, racial and tribal hatred, anger, bitterness, murder, and violence rule over the people. Until these spirits are bound, there can never be lasting peace in the Middle East. We will never be able to eliminate or annihilate terrorism without first binding up Satan's nefarious strongmen.

Before revival can come, the church must first bind up and defeat the ruler spirits assigned by Satan. So, let's review what we know.

Ephesians 6:12 says,

For we do not wrestle against flesh and blood, but against principalities, against powers, against the rulers of the darkness of this age, against spiritual hosts of wickedness in the heavenly places.

Therefore, we know that the battle is not against men but against the spirits controlling them. There are rulers of darkness roaming the earth, *"principalities," "powers,"* and *"rulers"* *(strongmen)* who exert control over much of the earth from the *"heavenly places."*

Jesus said, *"Or how can one enter a strong man's house and plunder his goods, unless he first binds the strong man? And then he will plunder his house"* (Matthew 12:29; see also Mark 3:27; Luke 11:21–22). We cannot set the captives free until we bind the strongmen over them. Many unbelievers will not accept the gospel until we take the blinders off them by binding up the spirits that are blinding them.

> *But even if our gospel is veiled, it is veiled to those who are perishing, whose minds the god of this age has blinded, who do not believe, lest the light of the gospel of the glory of Christ, who is the image of God, should shine on them.*
>
> (2 Corinthians 4:3–4)

This is not a new revelation. According to church expert C. Peter Wagner, except for Jesus Christ, South American pastor Carlos Annacondia is the greatest evangelist of all time, converting at least five thousand souls at every meeting.[12] Annacondia reports that before he goes into an area to conduct crusade meetings, he sends in teams to fast and pray in order to bind up the strongmen over that area. Only when God shows him that the strongmen are bound does Annacondia set up his crusade tents. Only then are the fields ripe for harvest!

> Many unbelievers will not accept the gospel until we take the blinders off them by binding up the spirits that are blinding them.

Other prophets and evangelists, such as Ed Silvoso and Cindy Jacobs, advocate a similar process.[13] They will send teams of intercessors who spend weeks fasting and praying against and binding up the strongmen over a city. Once the strongmen are bound, the teams then go in and evangelize the area with great success and with virtually no spiritual interference.

People often ask South Korean pastor David Yonggi Cho how his humble house church movement exploded into the largest church in the world. His answer has always been the same: "We bound up all of the strongmen over South Korea."

In the mid-1990s, I had the pleasure of teaching spiritual warfare in Fiji for six consecutive years. The church and Bible college where I taught arose early each morning to pray together and bind up the strongmen over Fiji. Today, there is a revival in Fiji and the church I ministered in is one of the mainstays of that revival.

I had the honor to teach on binding up the strongman in Sibu, a town in the Malaysian state of Sarawak, at the Sarawak Full Gospel Church's Bible College. The pastor there had spent twenty-six years building his church, which had three thousand members. When I returned the following year, the members gleefully told me that nine months earlier, they began binding up the strongmen over Sibu. When God told them that they had bound the strongmen, they went from house to house and converted two thousand more in just two weeks. They had to stop because they had no more room. When I returned around 1997, they had purchased a large parcel of land to build a church that would hold five thousand people in each service. Revival had sparked in Sibu.

THE KEYS TO THE KINGDOM

In Matthew 16:19, Jesus said to Peter, *"I will give you the keys of the kingdom of heaven, and whatever you bind on earth will be bound in heaven, and whatever you loose on earth will be loosed in heaven."* (See also Matthew 18:18.) We have the honor to

The Key to Revival: Spiritual Warfare

bind up the agents of Satan that govern much of the earth. The psalmist agrees:

> *Let the high praises of God be in their mouth, and a two-edged sword in their hand, to execute vengeance on the nations, and punishments on the peoples; to bind their kings with chains, and their nobles with fetters of iron; to execute on them the written judgment; this honor have all His saints. Praise the LORD!* (Psalm 149:6–9)

The word *loose* does not mean "to spread," as in "I loose the spirit of joy upon these people." It means "to break, shatter, or smash," as in shattering chains and breaking ropes.

Binding the strongmen is a simple prayer:

In the name of Jesus, I bind up the spirit of witchcraft (or any other strongman). I take chains from heaven and I bind you up hand and foot.

Many other variations are just as effective.

Group warfare can also take various forms. The two methods most often used involve a leader who does the initial praying. In one method, the leader might pray one sentence at a time, and the rest of the group echoes his prayer loudly:

Leader: "In the name of Jesus, I come against the spirit of witchcraft!"

Group: "In the name of Jesus, I come against the spirit of witchcraft!"

Leader: "I take chains from heaven and bind you up hand and foot."

Group: "I take chains from heaven and bind you up hand and foot."

And so forth.

In a second method, the leader prays continually to bind up ruler spirits and the rest of the group verbally agrees during his or her prayer by shouting, "Amen," "Alleluia," "Yes," or "We agree, Lord!"

THE POWER OF SHOUTING

When warring against the powers of darkness, the body of Christ must not be afraid to shout. Many Scripture passages in the Bible speak of shouting for joy whether in warfare prayer or in praising God.

> *"For He is good, for His mercy endures forever toward Israel." Then all the people shouted with a great shout, when they praised the LORD, because the foundation of the house of the LORD was laid.* (Ezra 3:11)

> *Sing, O daughter of Zion! Shout, O Israel! Be glad and rejoice with all your heart, O daughter of Jerusalem!* (Zephaniah 3:14)

The Lord God defeats His enemy with a roar:

> *The LORD shall go forth like a mighty man; He shall stir up His zeal like a man of war. He shall cry out, yes, shout aloud; He shall prevail against His enemies.* (Isaiah 42:13)

> *The LORD will roar from on high, and utter His voice from His holy habitation; He will roar mightily against His fold. He will give a shout, as those who tread the grapes, against all the inhabitants of the earth. A noise will come to the ends of the earth.* (Jeremiah 25:30–31)

The Key to Revival: Spiritual Warfare

God is a warrior who shouts and roars from His throne to destroy His enemies. God commands us to shout against Babylon, Satan's kingdom:

> *Put yourselves in array against Babylon all around, all you who bend the bow; shoot at her, spare no arrows, for she has sinned against the LORD.* **Shout against her all around.** (Jeremiah 50:14–15, emphasis added)

> *The LORD of hosts has sworn by Himself: "Surely I will fill you with men, as with locusts, and they shall lift up a shout against you."* (Jeremiah 51:14)

> *God has gone up with a shout.* (Psalm 47:5)

Jesus will shout when He returns: *"For the Lord Himself will descend from heaven with a shout"* (1 Thessalonians 4:16).

When Joshua and the nation of Israel went up against Jericho, God instructed them to walk once around the walled city without saying a word for six days in a row. On the seventh day they were to walk around Jericho seven times. After the seventh time, they were to *"shout with a great shout"* (Joshua 6:5). The walls of Jericho fell down immediately. (See verse 20.)

There is something powerful about shouting, both in the physical and the spiritual. Once, I went to Taiwan to observe their Independence Day celebrations. Five thousand men with large drums stood in a city square. On a signal, they pounded the drums and shouted at the top of their lungs. The sound was so deafening and penetrating that the hair on the back of my neck stood up and my heart began to race! I imagined an army going into battle with a great shout and roar. It was awesome! Shouting gives courage to soldiers and stirs them up. Shouting together brings the participants together in unity. The enemy, hearing the shouting, trembles with fear. Likewise, we are to shout praises to God as if the enemy is listening—because he is.

In our healing services, I can often recall how often God has inhabited the praises of His people as we have shouted, praised, and sung loudly in tongues. Some had visions and angelic visitations at such times. There is power in shouting, especially when praying against the enemy!

FIRST, BREAK THE CURSES

Before you can bind up ruler spirits, you must first break the curses that give evil spirits the right to rule. If curses are not broken, evil spirits have the right to oppress and you will not be able to bind them.

> Before you can bind up ruler spirits, you must first break the curses that give evil spirits the right to rule.

Some curses are brought about by our own sin and unrighteousness. When the sins of the people bring curses upon a land or nation, only confession and heartfelt repentance will break them. Therefore, the first step is to intercede, confess, and repent for the sins of the people. The prophet Daniel recognized the need to remove the curse on his people:

> *I, Daniel, understood by the books the number of the years specified by the word of the LORD through Jeremiah the prophet, that He would accomplish seventy years in the desolations of Jerusalem.* (Daniel 9:2)

The Key to Revival: Spiritual Warfare

Daniel knew that the seventy-year period of captivity in Babylon prophesied by Jeremiah was almost over. (See Jeremiah 25:11–12.) Therefore, he set himself to fast and pray for the liberation of God's people from Babylon. Even though the end of their captivity had been prophesied by Jeremiah, Daniel knew that God did nothing without someone first praying and crying out for it.

Daniel identified with the people and was a true intercessor as he confessed and repented of the sins of the people. Daniel continued, acknowledging that the sins of the people had brought curses upon them:

> *Yes, all Israel has transgressed Your law, and has departed so as not to obey Your voice; therefore the curse and the oath written in the Law of Moses the servant of God **have been poured out on us**, because we have sinned against Him.* (Daniel 9:11, emphasis added)

God forgave Judah, lifted the curses, and Cyrus of Persia liberated God's people from Babylon. Throughout the Bible, God's heart is always willing to forgive the repentant.

The good news is that Jesus Christ died on the cross, not only to break our curse, but also to serve as our curse:

> *Christ has redeemed us from the curse of the law, having become a curse for us (for it is written, "Cursed is everyone who hangs on a tree").* (Galatians 3:13).

DANIEL'S PRAYER

In April 2006, I was meditating on how revival could come to the Philippines. As I meditated, God instructed me to write a prayer patterned after Daniel's prayer in chapter

9. I will present it at the end of this book in both a long and short form.

I believe that if we, as a people, would begin to fast and pray Daniel's Prayer (or a similar prayer) daily, God will answer from heaven and move His hand of grace and mercy. God wants us to intercede, repent, break curses, and bind up Satan's ruler spirits.

THE COUNTERATTACKS OF SATAN

As you engage in spiritual warfare, Satan will likely launch some sort of counterattack against you. As I have experienced such attacks, God has shown me an important way you can protect yourself, your family, and your fellow church members.

Early in 2005, my assistant pastor's wife shared that she could not find her bank checkbook. It was usually in her purse. She emptied her purse three times and later handed it to her husband. He also searched through the purse but could not find the checkbook. In the end, she had to call her bank and place a stop order on her account. The next morning, as she was preparing to come to church, she opened her purse and there was the checkbook, sitting at the very top of all the items within.

A few weeks later, I went to my health insurance company to cancel my policy and switch to a less expensive plan. The agent asked for my Medicare card, which we are required to keep on us. I took my wallet out and could not find it. I emptied out all the contents on his desk and then asked my wife to look through it herself. It was not there. The next day, I opened my wallet, and there it was right in front of all my other cards.

The Key to Revival: Spiritual Warfare

A month later, I took my wife shopping at a membership discount store where entry is exclusive for cardholders. I told my wife to go first while I prayed in the car. An hour later, I went to meet her and I could not find my membership card. I stood at the door for fifteen minutes, going through my wallet very carefully. There was no card, and I had to wait outside for my wife. The next morning, I opened my wallet and my membership card was exactly where it had always been in my wallet!

I began to seriously pray and ponder over these strange events.

A few days later, I was cleaning my desk and came upon a book given to me five years before. My eyes fell on a chapter about avoiding Satan's counterattacks. The writer shared that God instructed him to pray Psalm 91 and ask Him to hide us under His wings and cover us with His feathers (see Psalm 91:4) so that the enemy cannot find or touch us.[14] It immediately resonated with me.

There had been events in the past where Satan attacked some of our members. God gave them Psalm 91 to pray and they made it through.

> *He is my refuge and my fortress; My God, in Him I will trust. Surely He shall deliver you from the snare of the fowler and from the perilous pestilence. He shall cover you with His feathers, and under His wings you shall take refuge; His truth shall be your shield and buckler.*
>
> (Psalm 91:2–4)

Pray daily that God will hide you and your family members under His wings and cover you with His feathers so that Satan cannot see you or touch you.

HOUSE CHURCHES FOR REVIVAL AND SURVIVAL

Once again in the Philippines, on the way up the mountain to the city of Baguio in 2000, God spoke to me and clearly said, "I want My church back!"

At first, I thought God wanted me to resign and give Him back my church. But God began to speak directly into my spirit and said that humankind had taken His church and turned it into man's church. Men had changed the structure, the practices, the doctrines, and the truth, twisting it to conform to man's ideas and philosophies in an attempt to wrestle authority away from God.

> God is leading His church back into homes and to the doctrines and practices taught by the early apostles.

For the first three hundred and twenty-five years of the church, there were no church buildings. God's people met in houses and in public areas. I believe that God is returning the concept of the house churches back to the body of Christ. He is looking for His pure church at the end times. Meanwhile, around the world, the house church movement is exploding![15]

The early church had no elite priesthood. Anyone who loved God, had some measure of spiritual maturity, knew the Word of God, and qualified under the guidelines found in 1 Timothy 3 could lead a group of believers in their house. During these times, Christianity grew and prospered during times of both persecution and peace.

The Key to Revival: Spiritual Warfare

The modern model for the house church is found in Mainland China. Despite intense persecution and even the threat of death, the underground house churches there have prospered. Today it is conservatively estimated that there are perhaps more than eighty million born-again Christians in China.[16]

If revival ignited today, existing church buildings would not be able to hold all the new converts. Even if money were available, land would have to be purchased, plans drawn, permits obtained, and ground broken. By the time that all occurred, the revival would probably be over. While ministering in Plovdiv, Bulgaria, recently, pastors informed me that the Bulgarian revival of 1990 to 1994 died because there were no more buildings to hold the new converts. I believe that God is leading His church back into homes and to the doctrines and practices taught by the early apostles.

This is not to say that returning to house churches is an easy task. It will take a lot of prayer and wisdom. Some may take advantage of the movement to divide churches by slipping in false teaching. Some may find themselves wandering aimlessly with no accountability. Still others may become mere social groups with a common interest. While there is the potential for abuse and the house church movement is suffering a fair amount of birth pangs, it is easy to see that sudden revival and the upcoming persecution will force the church to go underground and into house churches, like it or not.

THE PERFECTION OF THE SAINTS AND THE CHURCH

And He Himself gave some to be apostles, some prophets, some evangelists, and some pastors and teachers, for the equipping of the saints for the work of ministry, for the edifying of the body of Christ, till we all come to the unity of the faith and of the knowledge of the Son of God, to a perfect man, to the measure of the stature of the fullness of Christ; that we should no longer be children, tossed to and fro and carried about with every wind of doctrine, by the trickery of men, in the cunning craftiness of deceitful plotting.

(Ephesians 4:11–14)

From the very beginning, God wanted His children to be perfect—created in the image of His Son, Jesus. He also desired a perfect church without spot, wrinkle, or blemish (see Ephesians 5:27), prepared to become the bride of Christ when He returns. (See Revelation 21:2.) That is why He started the whole creation. Centuries later, He has not changed.

God is not going to bring the curtain down on planet earth before we meet His purpose. This does not mean that we have to be perfect in Christ at this very moment, but rather that the final touches will bring us to completion when He comes back.

We shall not all sleep, but we shall all be changed; in a moment, in the twinkling of an eye, at the last trumpet. For the trumpet will sound, and the dead will be raised incorruptible, and we shall be changed. For this corruptible must put on incorruption, and this mortal must put on immortality. So when this corruptible has put on incorruption, and this mortal has put on immortality, then shall be brought to pass the saying that is written: "Death is swallowed up in victory."

(1 Corinthians 15:51–54)

Before everything ends, God is going to have His overcomers, His remnant of true believers. (See Revelation 2:7, 11,

17, 26; 3:5, 12, 21.) As we fast and pray for revival, we need to continue to grow into spiritual maturity in Jesus Christ. That is God's desire and our goal.

Persecution will actually work to purge the church, helping to produce mature sons and daughters in the image of Jesus. (See Daniel 11:32–35.) Many will fall away, but out of them will emerge a faithful and mature remnant.

GOD'S END-TIME ARMY

In 1985, while praying early one morning, I had a vision of myself teaching a large group of soldiers in combat uniform. I heard a voice say, "Son, I want you to teach My army!" Since then, I have taught spiritual warfare, deliverance, and inner healing multiple times in Fiji, Vanuatu, Singapore, Sarawak, Hong Kong, mainland China, India, the Philippines, Switzerland, Bulgaria, and in the mainland United States. White horses and angels appear during some of the services and seminars, giving me the assurance that I am teaching God's army of the end times.

> As we fast and pray for revival, we need to continue to grow into spiritual maturity in Jesus Christ. That is God's desire and our goal.

Make no mistake, God is raising up an army for the end times that will engage the kingdom of darkness and fight on to victory. This is exciting news! Both Old and New Testaments speak of an army of God for the end times. In Joel, we find the following:

Blow the trumpet in Zion, and sound an alarm in My holy mountain! Let all the inhabitants of the land tremble; for the day of the LORD is coming, for it is at hand: a day of darkness and gloominess, a day of clouds and thick darkness, like the morning clouds spread over the mountains. A people come, great and strong, the like of whom has never been; nor will there ever be any such after them, even for many successive generations.

(Joel 2:1–2)

The *"day of the Lord"* will be the end of the world, the end of this age. When Jesus returns, it will be *"a day of darkness and gloominess, a day of clouds and thick darkness"* for much of the world. Or, as Jesus Himself described it:

The sun will be darkened, and the moon will not give its light; the stars will fall from heaven, and the powers of the heavens will be shaken. (Matthew 24:29)

The world and its inhabitants will tremble with fear. But in the midst of the darkness, an amazing thing will take place: a great multitude of people will appear on mount Zion as *"the morning clouds spread over the mountains"*—children of light, fully mature in Jesus Christ, and shining like the morning star. In Revelation, Jesus mentioned this star: *"And he who overcomes...I will give him the morning star"* (Revelation 2:26, 28). There has never been such a great and powerful people ever before and there will never be the like again! They will be invincible.

A fire devours before them, and behind them a flame burns; the land is like the Garden of Eden before them, and behind them a desolate wilderness; surely nothing shall escape them. (Joel 2:3)

The Key to Revival: Spiritual Warfare

God's end-time army will rise up to destroy all evil on the earth. It will be the final battle of this age between the kingdom of darkness and the kingdom of light.

> *And I saw the beast, the kings of the earth, and their armies, gathered together to make war against Him who sat on the horse and against His army. Then the beast was captured, and with him the false prophet who worked signs in his presence, by which he deceived those who received the mark of the beast and those who worshiped his image. These two were cast alive into the lake of fire burning with brimstone.*
> (Revelation 19:19–20)

No evil will escape them. They will be powerful and will not be defeated.

> *Their appearance is like the appearance of horses; and like swift steeds, so they run. With a noise like chariots over mountaintops they leap, like the noise of a flaming fire that devours the stubble, like a strong people set in battle array. Before them the people writhe in pain; all faces are drained of color.*
> (Joel 2:4–6)

Even as the prophet Elijah girded up his loins and ran past the chariot of Ahab (see 1 Kings 18:46), these mighty people of God will be faster and more powerful than horses. Did not Malachi 4:5 say that God was going to send *"Elijah the prophet before the coming of the great and dreadful day of the LORD"*? They will move as an army, *"a strong people set in battle array."*

These will not be ordinary people. They will be in perfect unity and obedience.

> *They run like mighty men, they climb the wall like men of war; every one marches in formation, and they do not break*

ranks. They do not push one another; every one marches in his own column. Though they lunge between the weapons, they are not cut down. (Joel 2:7–8)

Each will march on his own way and path and not another's. No one will try to do another person's job or strive to take someone else's rank or position. There will be no jealousy or envy. They will move in perfect harmony, unity, submission, and obedience, each doing the job that God gave him or her, focused on doing only His will. They will not betray one another. There will be no rebellion, no jealousy, and no backstabbing. They will not be wounded and will not die.

They run to and fro in the city, they run on the wall; they climb into the houses, they enter at the windows like a thief. The earth quakes before them, the heavens tremble; the sun and moon grow dark, and the stars diminish their brightness. (Joel 2:9–10)

Finally, verse 11 removes any doubt as to who these great people are:

*The LORD gives voice before **His army**, for His camp is very great; for strong is the One who executes His word. For the day of the LORD is great and very terrible; who can endure it?* (emphasis added)

Please understand, I am not advocating elitism in any form. God alone is the final arbiter and judge. All we can do is humble ourselves and submit ourselves to the Holy Spirit's leading.

CALLED TO THE FIGHT

God has called all of us as soldiers for Jesus:

The Key to Revival: Spiritual Warfare

You therefore must endure hardship as a good soldier of Jesus Christ. No one engaged in warfare entangles himself with the affairs of this life, that he may please him who enlisted him as a soldier. (2 Timothy 2:3–4)

Two hundred and forty-five times, God is referred to in Scripture as *"the Lord of hosts."* A *host* is an army. God has always said that we would be His instruments of warfare: *"You are My battle-ax and weapons of war: for with you I will break the nation in pieces; with you I will destroy kingdoms"* (Jeremiah 51:20).

Jesus did not come to bring peace on the earth; He came to defeat the kingdom of darkness in order to establish the kingdom of heaven on earth. *"For this purpose the Son of God was manifested, that He might destroy the works of the devil"* (1 John 3:8).

That is why we call Him the Lion of Judah. The devil resisted Him after His baptism in water. (See Luke 4:2–13.) The same thing is true for anyone who steps out to become a born-again Christian. The minute you enter into the kingdom of heaven, the devil comes to resist you. After your baptism in the Holy Spirit, you became a marked man or woman. The more you pray and fast and engage in spiritual warfare, the more the devil resists. The only solution is to go all the way and continue to fight against the devil. In the end, you cannot lose.

> The minute you enter into the kingdom of heaven, the devil comes to resist you. After your baptism in the Holy Spirit, you became a marked man or woman.

WAGING SPIRITUAL WARFARE

In 2 Timothy 4:7, the apostle Paul said, *"I have fought the good fight, I have finished the race, I have kept the faith."* Throughout his ministry of more than forty-five years, Paul fought against the powers of darkness and never lost.

The church is losing today because very few understand the need to go to war! Most Christians today are more like Cub Scouts than experienced soldiers, tamed house cats instead of lions of Judah. They avoid the battle and are therefore useless to the kingdom of God. Many have already become prisoners of war, bound by Satan.

CHAPTER EIGHT

THOSE WHO WILL ENDURE

According to Scripture, there are only two types of Christians who will endure. One will never die; the other type will give glory to God by willingly giving up their lives. *"But he who endures to the end shall be saved"* (Matthew 24:13).

THE WOMAN IN THE WILDERNESS

The apostle John wrote,

And there appeared a great wonder in heaven; a woman clothed with the sun, and the moon under her feet, and upon her head a crown of twelve stars: and she being with child cried, travailing in birth, and pained to be delivered.

(Revelation 12:1–2 KJV)

Who is this *"wonder in heaven"* shining like the sun? Many writers claim that she represents Israel, the nation that birthed the child who is Jesus. I disagree. In my opinion, this wonder

159

in heaven cannot be Israel, because when Jesus was born, Israel was far from being a *"wonder."* Israel was earthly, corrupt, immoral, and rebellious. On the contrary, Revelation compares Jerusalem to Sodom and Egypt:

> *And their dead bodies will lie in the street of the great city which spiritually is called Sodom and Egypt, where also our Lord was crucified.* (Revelation 11:8)

Israel was not clothed with the sun, and the moon was not under her feet; she was dark with sin and hypocrisy.

I believe that this woman, the great wonder in heaven, is the end-time true church of God—the bride of Christ. As we learned in the last chapter, God's true church of the end times will be made pure, comprising people who will be mature in the Spirit—true overcomers. That is why she shines like the sun. The moon is under her feet because she has defeated the kingdom of darkness and put it under her feet. The moon represents night and darkness—Satan's kingdom. With God's help, the true church will defeat Satan's demonic kingdom.

The crown of twelve stars refers to the twelve tribes of Israel. After Jesus ascended back into heaven, all true Christians became Jews in the spirit:

> *For he is not a Jew who is one outwardly, nor is circumcision that which is outward in the flesh but he is a Jew who is one inwardly; and circumcision is that of the heart, in the Spirit, not in the letter; whose praise is not from men but from God.* (Romans 2:28–29)

Galatians 6:15 confirms this: *"For in Christ Jesus neither circumcision nor uncircumcision avails anything, but a new creation."*

Those Who Will Endure

In Hosea 1:10, we find: *"And it shall come to pass in the place where it was said to them, 'You are not My people,' there it shall be said to them, 'You are sons of the living God.'"* Hosea 2:23 repeats that statement: *"Then I will say to those who were not My people, 'You are My people!' And they shall say, 'You are my God!'"*

Non-Jews, or Gentile Christians, have also become the people of God. As Paul was addressing the Romans, he said,

> *Even us whom He called, not of the Jews only, but also of the Gentiles? As He says also in Hosea: "I will call them My people, who were not My people, and her beloved, who was not beloved. And it shall come to pass in the place where it was said to them, 'You are not My people,' there they shall be called sons of the living God."*
>
> (Romans 9:24–26)

Thus, "spiritual Israel" is made up of all true Christians, both Jews and Gentiles.

The book of Revelation also identifies a great red dragon: *"And there appeared another wonder in heaven; and behold a great red dragon"* (Revelation 12:3 KJV). Later in this same chapter, the identity of this dragon is revealed as the devil—Satan. (See verse 9.) He is ready to devour the child that the woman (the true church) is about to birth.

THE MAN CHILD

Let's return again to the woman who is a wonder in heaven:

> *And she brought forth a man child, who was to rule all nations with a rod of iron: and her child was caught up unto God, and to his throne.* (Revelation 12:5 KJV)

Who is this *"man child"*? Is it Jesus, as many writers claim? Not in my opinion.

Jesus is described as one who would *"strike the nations. And He Himself will rule them with a rod of iron"* (Revelation 19:15), He will then give that honor to the overcomers.

Jesus did not flee to the throne of God to escape Satan. No, He defeated Satan and spoiled principalities, making a show of them openly, triumphing over them in it. (See Colossians 2:15.) When Jesus went to heaven, He went up in victory, not to escape the dragon. He was no child.

Revelation 2:26–27 says,

And he who overcomes, and keeps My works until the end, to him I will give power over the nations; "He shall rule them with a rod of iron; they shall be dashed to pieces like the potter's vessels"; as I also have received from My Father.

The man-child is the army of God, birthed by the true end-time church (the woman) and taken bodily up to the throne of God to escape the dragon. They will stand on Mount Zion, *"one hundred and forty-four thousand, having His Father's name written on their foreheads"* (Revelation 14:1). These are not angels; they are men and women *"redeemed from the earth"* (verse 3). They are not natural Israel; they are those who have been washed clean by the blood of Jesus. *"And in their mouth was found no deceit, for they are without fault before the throne of God"* (verse 5). They

> Satan wants us to think that we are weak and that he is as powerful as Jesus.
>
> **He is lying.**

will follow the Lamb wherever He goes. One day, they will come back with Jesus on white horses to destroy all evil on the face of the earth. (See Revelation 14:4; 19:14.)

Only God knows who will be counted in His true church, or His army, and who will become martyrs. For only God can look into our hearts and minds and judge by what He finds there.

Right now, Satan still controls much of the earth from the atmosphere around the earth. That is why the Bible calls him *"the prince of the power of the air"* (Ephesians 2:2). As stated earlier, Satan has appointed ruler spirits or strong-men to control much of our present world—every country, city, neighborhood, church, family, and person. He is still free to go to the very throne of God to accuse you and me. (See Revelation 12:10.)

Satan wants us to think that we are weak and that he is as powerful as Jesus. He is lying. Satan is afraid of the mature saints of God and will do anything to prevent them from believing and maturing. While we are to be aware Satan's power, we are not to be afraid of him.

His time has not yet come to be thrown down to earth. When that happens, however, it will not only be Michael and his angels warring against the demonic kingdom. The saints will be doing their part on earth, binding up Satan and his minions.

THE MARTYRS OF GOD

The other group to stand against the devil in the end times will be the martyrs of God.

And the dragon was enraged with the woman, and he went to make war with the rest of her offspring, who keep the commandments of God and have the testimony of Jesus Christ.   (Revelation 12:17)

They will testify powerfully during the three and a half years (the time of great revival), then Satan will kill them.

The tribulation will last for seven years. At the midpoint, Satan's beast will require every man, woman, and child to take the mark of the beast. To do that, they must renounce Jesus and their salvation. (See Revelation 14:9–11.) Decapitation awaits any who refuse. (See Revelation 13:15; 20:4.) The martyrs, or witnesses, will die at this point.

> Not all of us will die, but we all must be willing to die for the sake of the kingdom of God.

The witnesses will be very powerful, but will willingly die for the sake of Jesus' great name. They will bear witness that Christ died for us and lives in us. Like the Lord and the original disciples, they are not afraid to die for the truth. For them, *"to die is gain"* (Philippians 1:21). They will then rule the world with Christ:

> *Then I saw the souls of those who had been beheaded for their witness to Jesus and for the word of God, who had not worshiped the beast or his image, and had not received his mark on their foreheads or on their hands. And they lived and reigned with Christ for a thousand years.*
> (Revelation 20:4)

All believers who remain until the end will be willing to die for the sake of Jesus' great name. *"And they overcame him by the blood of the Lamb and by the word of their testimony, and they did not love their lives to the death"* (Revelation 12:11).

Not all of us will die, but we all must be willing to die for the sake of the kingdom of God.

CHAPTER NINE

A PEOPLE WHO WILL NEVER DIE

There will be people who will never die. They will go from life on earth to life eternal without dying. Revelation 12:6 says,

> And the woman [God's true, end-time church] *fled into the wilderness, where she hath a place prepared of God, that they should feed her there a thousand two hundred and threescore days.* (KJV)

"A thousand two hundred and threescore (sixty) days" is roughly three and a half years, or half of the tribulation. Those in the true church are destined to become the army of God, taken up to the throne of God to escape the dragon. *"And and her child was caught up unto God, and to his throne"* (verse 5 KJV).

> *These are the ones who follow the Lamb wherever He goes. These were redeemed from among men, being firstfruits to God and to the Lamb.* (Revelation 14:4)

167

This group of mature Christians will never see death. There may be others who will survive tribulation, but I personally doubt it.

In John 8:51, Jesus said, *"Most assuredly, I say to you, if anyone keeps My word he shall never see death."* Is Jesus saying that a man will die and rise again, or be resurrected after he dies? Neither. He is saying that a man who keeps His ways shall never see spiritual death—not once. I believe this is the generation that will fulfill that truth. Keep His truths in your heart.

> Outside of Jesus, there is no resurrection or eternal life. He has the keys to hell and death and the power to grant life and turn back death.

In John 11, Lazarus died and Jesus came to where Lazarus's two sisters lived, and where he lay in a tomb. Martha came out to meet him, and Jesus said to her,

"Your brother will rise again." Martha said to Him, "I know that he will rise again in the resurrection at the last day." Jesus said to her, "I am the resurrection and the life. He who believes in Me, though he may die, he shall live. And whoever lives and believes in Me shall never die. Do you believe this?" (John 11:23–26)

Jesus said: (1) *"He who believes in Me, **though he may die**, he shall live;"* and (2) *"**whoever lives** and believes in Me shall never die."*

Many Christians interpret the second part to mean a second death. However, Jesus clearly made a distinction between one who is dead and one who is living. Both resurrection and life are in Jesus. Outside of Jesus, there is no resurrection or eternal life. He has the keys to hell and death (see Revelation 1:18) and the power to grant life and turn back death.

God is raising up a people to defeat spiritual death. First Corinthians 15:24–26 says,

> *Then comes the end, when He delivers the kingdom to God the Father, when He puts an end to all rule and all authority and power. For He must reign till He has put all enemies under His feet. **The last enemy that will be destroyed is death.*** (emphasis added)

Raising the Dead

While ministering throughout the islands of Fiji for many years, I have run across several examples of the dead rising, just like Lazarus.

One evening, the local hospital phoned a member of the Fiji church and requested that she pick up the body of her young son who had died there that afternoon. She quickly called several other church members, and they prayed all night for her son to come back to life. The next morning she went to the hospital and found her son alive and well!

Another member of my church owned a local store. Two sisters, who were also Christians, came in, bought a few items, and left. A few minutes later, there was screaming in the parking lot. One of the sisters was on the ground, foaming at the mouth.

An ambulance arrived fifteen minutes later, but the woman had passed away. Despite this, the ambulance attendants spent another twenty minutes trying to resuscitate her. Eventually, they gave up and spent another ten minutes writing down information. Meanwhile, back in the store, the owner prayed that the woman would come back to life.

Later, she called me, saying, "Oh, I'm so disappointed. I prayed against the spirit of death and nothing happened."

"Well," I said, "maybe it wasn't God's will."

A month later, the owner received a phone call.

A woman said, "Do you remember the woman who died in your parking lot?"

"Yes," the owner replied.

"Can we come over?"

"Alright."

> It was the Holy Spirit who raised Christ from the dead, and He will raise us from the dead, too.

After she hung up, the owner said to herself, "What did she mean 'we'? One of them died!"

An hour later, the two sisters walked in. The woman who died had come back to life. She related how she was placed on a table in the hospital morgue and a physician verified that she was dead. As he was walking out of the room, she sat up. The physician almost died from fright. Her right arm was slightly paralyzed, and she had spent a month at the local rehabilitation center. As she stood in that store, however, she was in perfect health. Death had been defeated!

Make no mistake about it; the Holy Spirit raises the dead. We have no power in and of ourselves, but the Holy Spirit who

170

dwells in us does the work. It was the Holy Spirit who raised Christ from the dead, and He will raise us from the dead, too. (See Romans 8:11.)

Jesus said, *"I am the way, the truth, and the life"* (John 14:6). Leviticus 17 tells us: *"The life of the flesh is in the blood"* (verse 11). The life of Jesus is in His blood. There is power in the blood of Jesus, which gives life. Whenever you pray for the binding of death, pray the blood of Jesus.

ENOCH AND ELIJAH

In the Bible, there are two individuals who never died: Enoch and Elijah. In Genesis 5:24, we find: *"And Enoch walked with God; and he was not, for God took him."* God was pleased with Enoch and took him to heaven. Enoch never tasted death.

At the end of Elijah's ministry, Elisha, the servant of Elijah, followed him. *"Then it happened, as they continued on and talked, that suddenly a chariot of fire appeared with horses of fire, and separated the two of them; and Elijah went up by a whirlwind into heaven"* (2 Kings 2:11). Elijah never saw death.

The spirit of Elijah will return in the end times: *"I will send you Elijah the prophet before the coming of the great and dreadful day of the LORD"* (Malachi 4:5). Like John the Baptist, those with the spirit of Elijah will prepare the way of the Lord and make the crooked paths straight. They will push back the waters of death.

CHAPTER TEN

BEWARE OF FALSE REVIVAL

The coming revival will be both true and false at the same time. An identical thing happened in the days of King Josiah. The book of the law was discovered in the temple, and King Josiah did everything he could to restore true worship to the God of Israel. He destroyed all the pagan temples, killed the priests of Baal and Ashtoreth, and commanded that the nation observe God's holy festivals once again. The temples filled and the prophets and priests prospered.

> *Nevertheless the LORD did not turn from the fierceness of His great wrath, with which His anger was aroused against Judah, because of all the provocations with which Manasseh had provoked Him.* (2 Kings 23:26)

In the end, the Lord allowed Babylon to destroy Jerusalem, His great temple, and most of His people.

Why? Was not God pleased with the revival? No, God was angry. The revival was all smoke and shadow without substance. The temples became rich and people flocked to worship God, but it was all for show. They never changed their hearts nor went back to the old, true ways of God. It was not about God; it was about prosperity and the good life.

Let's return again to Jeremiah:

> *"Were they ashamed when they had committed abomination? No! They were not at all ashamed; nor did they know how to blush. Therefore they shall fall among those who fall; at the time I punish them, they shall be cast down," says the Lord. Thus says the Lord: "Stand in the ways and see, and ask for the old paths, where the good way is, and walk in it; then you will find rest for your souls. But they said, 'We will not walk in it.'"* (Jeremiah 6:15–16)

The people continued to compromise true worship to the one and only God of the universe. On one hand, they made a show of attending temple functions; on the other hand, they worshipped and observed Babylonian religious customs. They continued to worship the "Queen of Heaven" and to *"pour out drink offerings to other gods, that they may provoke Me to anger"* (Jeremiah 7:18). They gave lip service to the Word of God and His laws.

Jeremiah went around warning of war, but no one listened. His heart was pained and he could not hold back any longer. He spoke out against the prophets and priests who, in turn, wanted to kill him for speaking the truth. They were blind to their own sins.

> *And it shall be, when you show this people all these words, and they say to you, "Why has the Lord pronounced all this great disaster against us? Or what is our iniquity? Or*

what is our sin that we have committed against the LORD
our God?" (Jeremiah 16:10)

Repeatedly he warned them, but they refused to listen.
Life was just too good. The revival, however, was a counterfeit
revival! In the end, only Jeremiah
and a few others survived the war.
But the same principles apply to
us today.

Today, some pastors are using
"Madison Avenue" public rela-
tions techniques to impress the
crowd. There are television preachers promising that if you accept
Jesus He will bless you and give
you everything you ever wanted
in life. There are "mega-churches"
filled with tens of thousands of
people who get what they want,
not what they need. Their leaders
think, *Keep the people happy. Don't
preach repentance, judgment, or sac-
rifice. Those themes will drive people away.* The pressure to draw
and keep big crowds, maintain huge budgets, and be recognized by others as a "successful church" has led some to compromise the message of the cross.

> The pressure to draw big crowds, maintain huge budgets, and be recognized by others as "successful" has led some to compromise the message of the cross.

God is upset today, too. His wrath will not be turned
away.

In Ezekiel 9, God commanded six angels with weapons
in their hands to come forth. One of them had an inkhorn
by his side. He commanded the one with the inkhorn as
follows:

> *"Go through the midst of the city, through the midst of Jerusalem, and **put a mark on the foreheads** of the men who sigh and cry over all the abominations that are done within it."* To the others He said in my hearing, *"Go after him through the city and kill; do not let your eye spare, nor have any pity. Utterly slay old and young men, maidens and little children and women; but **do not come near anyone on whom is the mark**; and begin at My sanctuary."* So they began with the elders who were before the temple. Then He said to them, *"Defile the temple, and fill the courts with the slain. Go out!"* And they went out and killed in the city.
>
> (Ezekiel 9:4–7, emphasis added)

This is important. God commanded that only those who *"sigh and cry"* because of what was going on in His temple would receive a mark on their foreheads. All others would perish. Destruction and judgment begins with the church.

How interesting that in the end times, God will also signify His true servants with His mark on their foreheads. In Revelation 7, four angels were commanded to harm the earth and the sea. However, before they could proceed, another angel came and declared, *"Do not harm the earth, the sea, or the trees till we have sealed the servants of our God on their foreheads"* (verse 3). These were to be spared.

In Revelation 9, destruction was coming to earth once more. *"They were commanded not to harm the grass of the earth, or any green thing, or any tree, but only those men who do not have the seal of God on their foreheads"* (verse 4).

God has not changed. His wrath is still on those who worship other gods and goddesses, observe heathen religious practices, and fornicate with other religions and compromise the Word of God.

Jeremiah went around crying:

Thus says the LORD of hosts, the God of Israel: "Amend your ways and your doings, and I will cause you to dwell in this place. Do not trust in these lying words, saying, 'The temple of the LORD'....Behold, you trust in lying words that cannot profit." (Jeremiah 7:3–4, 8)

God will bring judgment on His backslidden people one more time. Destruction is coming to the body of Christ, but God will have His remnant—His true church, His army, and His martyrs—to the end. Throughout Scripture, God has demonstrated that if we are disobedient and rebellious, He will allow the enemy to destroy His temple, His city, and most of His people in order to purge them.

> God has demonstrated that if we are disobedient and rebellious, He will allow the enemy to destroy His temple and most of His people in order to purge them.

As in Jeremiah's day, so much of our worship of God today is shallow and superficial. Few understand or care about what is going on in the spiritual realm. Many so-called Christians have never truly surrendered their lives to God. They give lip service to God on Sunday but are still bound to the world the rest of the week. Many do not believe that Satan or demons exist. Some churches are compromising the true gospel of the kingdom until it is barely recognizable. Too many Christians do not even know that we are already in a war. Multitudes could not care less.

As in Noah's day, the storm clouds are gathering, or, as Jesus said,

> *But as the days of Noah were, so also will the coming of the Son of Man be. For as in the days before the flood, they were eating and drinking, marrying and giving in marriage, until the day that Noah entered the ark, and did not know until the flood came and took them all away, so also will the coming of the Son of Man be.* (Matthew 24:37–39)

Christianity in Europe has faded into complete irrelevance. Low birth rates and steadily increasing immigration from the Middle East has seen Islam completely overwhelm Christianity. In Germany, home of Martin Luther and the reformation, as well as in many ex-Soviet countries, there has been an explosion of interest in witchcraft and the occult. Denominational and church growth in the United States is on the sharp decline as well.

It is the modern day Judah of Jeremiah's era. In Jeremiah 4:16–18, God says,

> *"Make mention to the nations, yes, proclaim against Jerusalem, that watchers come from a far country and raise their voice against the cities of Judah. Like keepers of a field they are against her all around, because she has been rebellious against Me,"* says the LORD. *"Your ways and your doings have procured these things for you. This is your wickedness, because it is bitter, because it reaches to your heart."*

America has turned its back to God, and nations all over the world are taking joy in watching her apparently approaching demise. They work and plot against her and are jealous of her prosperity. With glee, they are watching America fall. The curse is on the land and people. Part of the coming revival will be as shallow as that of Jeremiah's day.

DIVISION IN THE BODY

Denominations will not likely change in the coming revival. If history is any indication, they will probably cling to pet doctrines and continue their divisive ways. They may even increase in numbers during the coming revival, but disunity within the body of Christ will continue. Whatever unity there is will be only fragile and surface.

Many saints will join the one-world religion. They will abandon the faith to fight against Christianity and against Christians who they feel lied and misled them. Former Christians will be some of our worst enemies.

When China opened up to the West, many denominations entered and established underground house churches there. Previously, the vast majority of Chinese house churches were independent. Now, many recent accounts report fighting among denominational house churches and others. One news article published by *The Martyrs' Cry* claims that house churches of one denomination fought openly with other house churches, killing several and injuring many. The government subsequently clamped down harder on Christianity, calling Christians a bunch of violent, murderous criminals.

THE POINT

A great harvest is coming, but there will be two sides to it. There will be true revival, but there will also be a false one. Be aware. In the end, those involved in the false revival will fall to Satan's beast.

CHAPTER ELEVEN

ENGAGING THE ENEMY

ealing, deliverance, prayer, knowing God's Word, evangelism—these are just some of the crucial things we as Christians are called to do as part of our war against Satan's kingdom. It is our role in spiritual warfare by which we can help take back territory from Satan. Almighty God, however, is interested in total victory.

THE NECESSITY OF PRAYER

God intends His church to be a house of prayer. (See Isaiah 56:7.) Prayer is fundamental to the kingdom of God. It is essential and effective in moving the hand of God. It is not an optional activity but rather our primary weapon in the war against Satan's kingdom. Without prayer, the war is lost!

With prayer, we become coworkers—and co-warriors—with God. God's purposes are carried out through the prayers of the saints. It is God who prompts us to pray and it is the Holy Spirit who takes our prayers and intercedes for us.

Likewise the Spirit also helps in our weaknesses. For we do not know what we should pray for as we ought, but the Spirit Himself makes intercession for us with groanings which cannot be uttered. (Romans 8:26)

The *Amplified Bible* puts it this way:

So too the (Holy) Spirit comes to our aid and bears us up in our weakness; for we do not know what prayer to offer nor how to offer it worthily as we ought, but the Spirit Himself goes to meet our supplication and pleads in our behalf with unspeakable yearnings and groanings too deep for utterance.

At the end of the world, the prayers of the saints will be crucial. In Revelation 6 and 7, great judgment falls on earth with incredible power. It is released by the Lord Jesus Christ, who is the only one able to take the book and release each seal. Revelation 5:8 says,

Now when He had taken the scroll, the four living creatures and the twenty-four elders fell down before the Lamb, each having a harp, and golden bowls full of incense, **which are the prayers of the saints.** (emphasis added)

As each of the first six seals is opened, the final stages unfold as great judgment and calamities shake the earth. The prayers of the saints come to remembrance, and the Lord Jesus both protects His saints on earth and punishes their enemies. The breaking of each seal brings increasingly greater destruction.

When the seventh seal is about to be opened, Scripture says,

When He opened the seventh seal, there was silence in heaven for about half an hour. And I saw the seven angels

who stand before God, and to them were given seven trumpets. Then another angel, having a golden censer, came and stood at the altar. He was given much incense, that he should offer it with the prayers of all the saints upon the golden altar which was before the throne. And the smoke of the incense, with the prayers of the saints, ascended before God from the angel's hand.

(Revelation 8:1–4, emphasis added)

There is tremendous power and authority in the prayers of the saints. What do these prayers do? They remind God of His saints and elicit mercy and grace from Him.

> There is tremendous power and authority in the prayers of the saints.

In the days of Moses, Korah and his two hundred and fifty men of renown rebelled against Moses and Aaron:

Korah gathered all the congregation against them at the door of the tabernacle of meeting. Then the glory of the Lord appeared to all the congregation. And the Lord spoke to Moses and Aaron, saying, "Separate yourselves from among this congregation, that I may consume them in a moment."

(Numbers 16:19–21)

But Moses and Aaron prayed that God would have mercy and spare all those who separated themselves from Korah and his men. Their prayers were answered. God judged Korah and his men and the earth opened and swallowed them up, their houses, all the men that were with Korah, and all their goods. (See verse 32.)

Even after all that, the congregation still murmured against Moses and Aaron. *"And the LORD spoke to Moses, saying, 'Get away from among this congregation, that I may consume them in a moment'"* (Numbers 16:44–45). Moses and Aaron fell on their faces.

> So Moses said to Aaron, "Take a censer and put fire in it from the altar, put incense on it, and take it quickly to the congregation and make atonement for them; for wrath has gone out from the LORD. The plague has begun." Then Aaron took it as Moses commanded, and ran into the midst of the assembly; and already the plague had begun among the people. So he put in the incense and made atonement for the people. And he stood between the dead and the living; so the plague was stopped.
>
> (verses 46–48)

The incense reminded God of the prayers of Moses and Aaron, and God had mercy and stopped the plague. The prayers of God's people will stay His mighty hand. Otherwise, He would probably consume the entire earth in His wrath. Our prayers have an effect in heaven.

TRUE UNITY

There is power in agreement, or unity. When two pray together, the power increases tenfold. Only through prayer can *"one chase a thousand, and two put ten thousand to flight"* (Deuteronomy 32:30). It is a spiritual principle. Satan's demons have power. On our own, we are no match for Satan's strongmen. Their power, however, is no match for the power of God. Even one church fighting alone would have a difficult time, depending on the strength of the ruler spirit assigned by Satan. True, a few individuals acting alone may possess enough spiritual power to confront ruler spirits by themselves. However, they would still be inadequate to spark worldwide revival.

It is vital that churches come together to pray against Satan's ruler spirits. The more that churches pray to bind ruler spirits, the more likely is their success. If churches all over the world would begin praying for one another and binding the ruler spirits over areas around the world, the power released would be incredible.

> If churches all over the world begin praying for one another and binding the ruler spirits over areas around the world, the power will be incredible.

When one church fights against Satan's demonic kingdom, he can muster his troops against that church, but if many churches begin to pray to bind up spirits in other countries around the world, he cannot shut everyone up. Imagine a few hundred or even thousands of churches all over the world binding up ruler spirits over your church or country. Prayers against his ruler spirits would come from all directions and the spiritual power they release would be exceedingly powerful.

It is imperative that we join in binding up Satan's ruler spirits over the Philippines, Fiji, Vanuatu, Singapore, Switzerland, Bulgaria, Hong Kong, China, Australia, New Zealand, the United States, and all over the world. Pray for us and we will pray for you.

185

Let us rise up as a mighty army of God! Please pray Daniel's Prayer every day and join the body of Christ in fasting and praying every Friday from this day forth. Fast all day and pray all night, or some portion of the day as the Holy Spirit leads. Take the initiative and invite churches in your area and in other countries to pray for and bind up ruler spirits over those countries. Let us go back to God's ways. Let us be the generation that will give God back His church!

Let us grow up to maturity in the Lord and begin to fight back!

Let us be God's army and move the hand of God to bring revival and the end of evil on earth!

SUMMARY

In summary, allow us to point out the following:

1. It has been prophesied many times that the last and greatest revival of all time would start in the northern provinces of the Philippines. A vision and an angel appeared to me in Lal-lo to confirm it.

2. The coming revival will be far greater than all previous revivals put together, in terms of both scope and time. Its numbers will be in the millions.

3. Satan is going to resist this coming revival with everything that he has because he knows that it means the end of his kingdom and reign on earth. He will be thrown into the bottomless pit and then cast into the Lake of Fire. (See Revelation 20:1-2; 10.) Already, he is forming the one-world government and the one-world religion spoken of in Revelation 13.

4. The coming revival will mark the end of the world, or the end of this age.

5. The Bible says that Satan's beast is going to war against the saints and overcome them. (See Revelation 13:7; Daniel 7:21, 25.)

6. The great revival will result in intense persecution and the abomination of desolation spoken of by Daniel the prophet.

7. We are already in a war and under the widespread deception spoken of by the Lord in Matthew 24:11, 24. Many have joined ecumenical movements and are compromising the gospel already. They preach prosperity instead of sacrifice. They allow sin and deception into the church.

8. The apostles clearly warned us not to accept a different Jesus or any gospel not taught by the original apostles. We are not to compromise.

9. The key to revival is spiritual warfare—repentance, breaking curses, and binding up Satan's strongmen. The example and model is Daniel's prayer in Daniel 9. The body of Christ needs to pray together in unity for each other and revival.

10. We can block Satan's counterattacks by praying Psalm 91.

11. God wants us to return to the ways of the early church—practicing its original and pure doctrines and meeting in house churches in order to sustain revival and resist persecution.

12. Revival and the end of the world will not come until God's perfect sons and daughters, as well as His Church, are without spot, wrinkle, or blemish. During all of this, maturity in Jesus Christ must continue. We are in a race to perfection!

13. Before the end, God's overcomers—His true church, the army of God—will emerge. Those who are martyred for His sake will receive their heavenly reward. Those in God's true church, who are taken up to His heavenly throne, will never die but will return with Christ in glory to take their stand and fight against Satan in the final battle.

14. As in the book of Jeremiah, there will be both a true and false revival. Do not be fooled! Do not allow deception to seep in and corrupt the church. God is looking for those who will fast and pray, and who will worship Him in spirit and in truth.

15. If the body of Christ will humble itself and pray together to confess and repent for the sins of the people, God will forgive us, break the curses, and give us the right and the power to bind up ruler spirits. When the strong-men over cities and countries around the world are bound, revival will take place.

Let us bind our hearts together and pray to bind up all of the ruler spirits over every area of the world. Let us not stand idly by and do nothing.

A CALL TO ARMS

Revival must come; it is ordained by God and predicted by the prophets in Scripture.

Surely, there are faithful and diligent Christians who are willing to come together in prayer to fight for revival! While we are praying and waiting on God for revival, He is waiting for us to war against the demonic kingdom and to mature in Jesus Christ. Christians everywhere need to take a stand and help bind up the ruler spirits of deception, idolatry, thievery, corruption, pride, poverty, greed, antichrist, witchcraft,

Engaging the Enemy

Jezebel and Ahab, slavery, lust, sexual immorality, violence, murder, hatred, anger, religiosity, and so forth, over the Philippines and over the rest of the world.

Let us go to war!

DANIEL'S PRAYER
(Based on Daniel 9)

Pray this prayer every time the saints come together and individually, daily:

Father, we come to You in the name of our Lord and Savior, Jesus Christ.

1. O Lord, righteousness belongs to You, but we are ashamed. We, Your people all over the world, have sinned against You.

2. We confess our sins and the sins of our forefathers. We have sinned against You. We have lived wickedly, and have rebelled, disobeying Your voice and Your will.

3. We have allowed ourselves to be deceived and distracted.

4. We have not walked with the Holy Spirit, whom You gave us to guide us, teach us, and show us all truth. We have become spiritually immature, worldly, and unable to live out the truth. We have failed to do Your will.

5. We confess and repent of the sins of idolatry, witchcraft, sexual immorality, theft, lying, greed, pride, murder, adultery,

dishonoring our parents, unbelief, lack of love, and countless other sins against You, O Lord.

6. Because of our sins and disobedience, our land and people have been cursed.

7. But You are a merciful God, full of grace and love, and we ask that You forgive us our sins and cleanse us of all unrighteousness.

8. O Lord, hear our prayers, open Your eyes, and see our despair.

9. O Lord, hear! O Lord, forgive! O Lord, listen and act! Do not delay for Your own sake, my God, for Your people are called by Your name. Break the curses that have come upon our land and people, we humbly ask, O God.

10. We bind all ruler spirits Satan has sent to carry out those curses against us, in Jesus' name. Your Word says whatever we bind on earth will be bound in heaven, and whatever we loose on earth will be loosed in heaven. [See Matthew 16:19; 18:18.] Free the souls of men, women, and children who have been bound by Satan, and take the blinders off their minds. We humbly ask You to send angels with chains from heaven to bind up all of Satan's ruler spirits that control our land and people.

11. We cut off all of the cords of the enemy and cast them away.

12. Hide us beneath Your wings and cover us with Your feathers to protect us against the enemy. *"He will cover you with his feathers, and under his wings you will find refuge"* (Psalm 91:4).

We give You all the praise and honor and glory, O Lord God. In Jesus' name we pray, amen.

DANIEL'S PRAYER
(SHORT VERSION)
(Based on Daniel 9)

Father, we come to You in the name of our Lord and Savior, Jesus Christ.

1. O Lord, righteousness belongs to You, but we are ashamed. We, Your people all over the world, have sinned against You.

2. We confess and repent of our sins, for we have rebelled against You and have disobeyed Your commandments.

3. We have committed sins of idolatry, witchcraft, sexual immorality, theft, lying, greed, pride, murder, adultery, dishonoring our parents, unbelief, lack of love, and countless other sins against You, O Lord.

4. Because of our sins, curses have come upon the land and upon Your people.

5. We are deceived, weak, carnal, and divided. We fail to love others. We have failed to do Your will. Satan has us bound.

6. We humbly pray for forgiveness for our sins, our transgressions, and our iniquities, O Lord. We have no righteousness of our own, but we come in the name of Jesus and His righteousness and grace. Have mercy on us, O God.

7. Break the curses that came upon us because of our sins, O Lord. We are not worthy, but You are full of grace and mercy, O God. Forgive Your children.

8. We bind up the ruler spirits Satan has set over our land and people and we cut off their cords, in Jesus' name.

8. We loose the souls of men, women, and children and take away the blindness of their minds.

9. Hide us under Your wings and cover us with Your feathers, O Lord.

In Jesus' name we pray, amen.

ENDNOTES

CHAPTER ONE

[1] Charles H. Kraft, *Defeating Dark Angels*. Ann Arbor, MI: Vine Books, 1992.

CHAPTER TWO

[2] For a fuller discussion on the dangers of applying inner healing and deliverance at the wrong times, I recommend *A Comprehensive Guide to Deliverance and Inner Healing* by John and Mark Sandford. (See additional resources.)

[3] Penfield, Wilder. *The Mystery of the Mind: A Critical Study of Consciousness and the Human Brain*. Princeton, NJ: Princeton University Press, 1975.

CHAPTER THREE

[4] Hammond, Frank and Ida Mae. *Pigs in the Parlor*. Kirkwood, MO: Impact Books, Inc., 1993.

CHAPTER FOUR

[5] For a full explanation and defense of how and why Christians can have demons, see the first chapter of my first

book, Ing, Richard. *Spiritual Warfare*. New Kensington, PA: Whitaker House, 1996.

CHAPTER FIVE

[6] Buck, Roland H. *Angels on Assignment*. New Kensington, PA: Whitaker House, 1979.

CHAPTER SIX

[7] Nee, Watchman. *The Spirit of Wisdom and Revelation*. New York, NY: Christian Fellowship Publishers, 1980.

[8] Hunt, Dave. *Global Peace*. Eugene, OR: Harvest House, 1990.

[9] Hattaway, Paul. *Operation China*. Bartlesville, OK: The Voice of the Martyrs, 2000.

[10] Various polls published on www.barna.org. Or see: Barna, George. *Growing True Disciples*. Colorado Springs, CO: Water Brook Press, 2001.

[11] MacArthur, John. *Hard to Believe: The High Cost and Infinite value of Following Jesus*. Nashville, TN: Thomas Nelson, Inc. 2003.

CHAPTER SEVEN

[12] Wagner, C. Peter. *The Third Wave of the Holy Spirit*. Ann Arbor, MI: Servant Books, 1988.

[13] See articles by C. Peter Wagner and Ed Silvoso in Ted Haggard and Jack Hayford's *Loving Your City into the Kingdom*. Ventura, CA: Regal Books, 1997.

[14] Jackson, John Paul. *Needless Casualties of War*. Ft. Worth, TX: Streams Publications, 1999.

Endnotes

[15] Rutz, James. *Megashift: Igniting Spiritual Power.* Colorado Springs, CO: Empowerment Press, 2005.

[16] Aikman, David. *Jesus in Beijing.* Washington, D.C.: Regnery Publishing, Inc., 2003.

ADDITIONAL RESOURCES

John and Mark Sandford. *A Comprehensive Guide to Deliverance and Inner Healing*. Grand Rapids, MI: Baker, 1992.

Dr. Neil Anderson. *Released from Bondage*. Nashville, TN: Thomas Nelson, 2002.

Charles H. Kraft. *Deep Wounds, Deep Healing*. Ventura, CA: Regal Books, 1993.

_____, *Defeating Dark Angels*. Ventura, CA: Regal Books, 1992.

Trevor Dearing. *God and Healing of the Mind*. Martley, England: Crossbridge Books, 2006.

ABOUT THE AUTHOR

D r. Richard Ing is the senior pastor of Light of the World Missions in Hawaii and the Philippines. He holds a Doctor of Ministry degree and is vice president of New Covenant International Seminary and Bible College. Dr. Ing also operates a Bible college, mission house, and vocational training center in the Philippines. He has lectured frequently on spiritual warfare in Fiji, Vanuatu, India, mainland China, Hong Kong, Singapore, Sarawak, Bulgaria, and the Philippines, as well as the US mainland.

Dr. Ing was a civil engineer before graduating from Hastings College of the Law in San Francisco. He recently retired from law practice after forty years. Married for more than forty years, Dr. Ing has four children and resides in Hawaii, where he was born and raised.

Spiritual Warfare
Richard Ing

In this powerful examination of spiritual warfare, Richard Ing discusses the rulers and hierarchies of the demonic kingdom. He reveals the Jezebel and Ahab spirits that plague today's church, destroying even the most effective ministries through controlling women and passive men. Discover how to overcome Satan's insidious tactics by learning the techniques and strategies available in your full arsenal of weapons, including the proper use of binding and loosening. Victorious spiritual warfare is yours as the Holy Spirit empowers you in the body of Christ!

ISBN: 978-0-88368-917-2 • Trade • 304 pages

WHITAKER
HOUSE

www.whitakerhouse.com

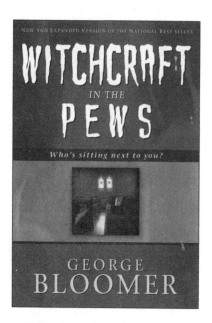

**Witchcraft in the Pews
(revised and expanded edition)**
George Bloomer

Awaken, church! The enemy is within! With this powerful and explosive book, Bishop George Bloomer exposes the shocking truth about witchcraft and occultic practices within the Christian church. As Satan's diabolical schemes have grown more intense, his reach has infiltrated America's pulpits and pews. Discover how some ministers use intimidation and fear against their own congregations. Find out how to resist controlling and abusive authority figures. Grow in your discernment as you get free and stay free in Jesus Christ. It's time for the church to take a stand and position itself for the victory that Christ has already won!

ISBN: 978-1-60374-033-3 • Hardcover • 176 pages

WHITAKER HOUSE

www.whitakerhouse.com

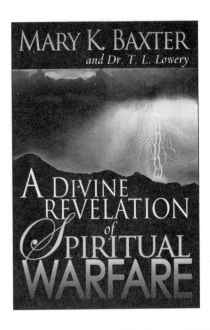

A Divine Revelation of Spiritual Wafare

Mary K. Baxter
with Dr. T. L. Lowery

Best-selling author Mary K. Baxter has learned the secrets
of applying Christ's victory and defeating both sin and Satan.
In these pages, you'll learn how to receive divine protection
and use the spiritual weapons that are rightfully yours as a
child of God. The enemy seeks to conquer and destroy your
spirit, soul, and body! Yet the devil has far less power than
God has given to us. Find out how you can participate
in Christ's victory over the enemy right now
and live a victorious life!

ISBN: 978-0-88368-694-2 • Trade • 208 pages

WHITAKER
HOUSE

www.whitakerhouse.com

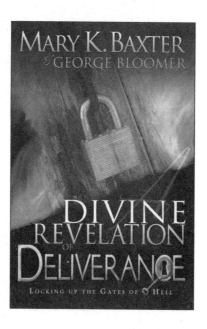

A Divine Revelation of Deliverance
Mary K. Baxter
with George Bloomer

Many Christians live with frustration and defeat. They
wonder why they can't overcome sins and temptations,
even though they pray and try to be strong. Yet God loves
us and wants to set us free. Through Christ, He gives us
victory over the enemy and the power to deliver others
who are pawns of Satan's destructive plans. Mary K. Baxter
exposes Satan's schemes and provides much-needed hope
for the suffering and oppressed. Receive a divine
revelation of your deliverance in Christ!

ISBN: 978-0-88368-754-3 • Trade • 224 pages

www.whitakerhouse.com

Free at Last:
Removing the Past from Your Future
(with Study Guide CD)
Larry Huch

You can break free from your past! Don't let what has happened to you and your family hold you back in life. You can find freedom from depression, anger, abuse, insecurity, and addiction in Jesus Christ. Pastor Larry Huch reveals powerful truths from Scripture that enabled him and many others to quickly break the destructive chains in their lives and receive God's blessings. Learn the secret to true freedom and you, too, can regain your joy and hope, experience divine health, mend broken relationships, walk in true prosperity—body, soul, and spirit.

ISBN: 978-0-88368-428-3 • Trade with CD • 272 pages

www.whitakerhouse.com

Lucifer Exposed:
The Devil's Plan to Destroy Your Life
Derek Prince

Satan, the fallen archangel, desires nothing more than to win the loyalty, hearts, and minds of the entire human race—and he won't quit in his attempt to win you over! Derek Prince uncovers Satan's greatest weapon in enslaving the average person into bondage. Satan attempts to seduce Christians from rising to their full potential and to distract every human being from following God. Are you—or someone you know—struggling with abuse, pornography, addiction, gluttony, or other issues? Use the mighty spiritual weapons revealed in this compelling book, and victory can be yours!

ISBN: 978-0-88368-836-6 • Trade • 160 pages

WHITAKER
HOUSE

www.whitakerhouse.com

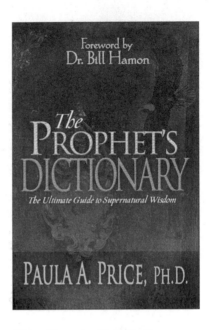

The Prophet's Dictionary:
The Ultimate Guide to Supernatural Wisdom
Paula A. Price

The Prophet's Dictionary by Paula Price is an essential tool for laymen, prophets, prophesiers, pastors, intercessors, and dreamers of dreams. As the ultimate all-in-one dictionary and reference book, it contains over 1600 relevant definitions of terms and phrases for the prophetic realm of Christian ministry. Here you will discover how to correctly interpret and apply God's prophetic words, distinguish between true and false prophets, understand God-given dreams, and develop your spiritual gifts. Also included are prophetic visions and clues to interpreting their symbolism, imagery, and signs.

This one-of-a-kind resource is a book no Christian should be without!

Hardcover ISBN: 978-1-60374-035-7 • Trade Paper ISBN: 978-0-88368-999-8

WHITAKER
HOUSE

www.whitakerhouse.com